17954

D0399421

Great
upon
the
mountain

Vinson Brown

Great upon the mountain

The story of
Crazy Horse,
legendary mystic
and warrior

MACMILLAN PUBLISHING CO., INC.
New York
COLLIER MACMILLAN PUBLISHERS
London

Macmillan Publishing Co., Inc.
866 Third Avenue,
New York, N. Y. 10022
Collier-Macmillan Canada Ltd.

Great upon the Mountain was
originally published by Nature-
graph Publishers, and is reprinted
by agreement.

Map by Clarice Borio

Library of Congress Cataloging in Publication Data

Brown, Vinson, 1912-
    Great upon the mountain.

    Bibliography: p.
    1. Crazy Horse, Oglala Indian, 1842 (ca.)-1877.
I. Title.
E99.'3C722   1975   970.3 [B]   74-13458
ISBN 0-02-517350-2

First Printing 1975

*Printed in the United States of
America*

Acknowledgments

The author wishes to express his grateful
appreciation to the following persons for their
kind suggestions, criticisms, and other help in
the completion of this book: to Chio Jari, the
Guaymi Indian youth who first gave the author
an inkling of the great spiritual quality of a
Native American religion; to Peter Blue Cloud
(Mohawk) for his helpful criticisms of the
manuscript; to Jean Leonard (Editor of *The
Great Plains Observer*) for her splendid work in
editing and typing the final manuscript, and
her added suggestions of ways to improve the
book; to Frank Fools Crow (medicine man on
the Pine Ridge Reservation in South Dakota)
for his spiritual inspiration and his stories, told
him by his grandfather, about Crazy Horse; to
Charles Fire Thunder (of the same reservation)
for his accounts (told him by both his father
and grandfather) of the life of Crazy Horse; to
the late Mari Sandoz, author of *Crazy Horse*,

Strange Man of the Oglala, for the inspiration and helpful details of her book, which are sometimes paraphrased in this book, though without any intent to copy; to Red Dawn (Stephen Jones, Jr., Santee Sioux) for his reading of the manuscript and fine Foreword for this book; to David Moore, an outstanding youth, whose deep spiritual affinity with and interest in the American Indians was the inspiration for the character of Bear Boy; to Korczak Ziolkowski, for the inspiration of his magnificent sculpturing of Crazy Horse on Thunderhead Mountain in the Black Hills and his kindness in taking the author up on the mountain itself; to his wife, Ruth, for kindly proofreading the article on the Crazy Horse Monument; and, finally, to the three allied tribes, the Lakota (or Sioux), the Cheyennes, and the Arapahoes, whose spirit and example in bravely resisting a ruthless and unprincipled conquest demonstrated the strength of Indian character and the nobility of their cause.

This book is dedicated to my son,
Keven, who shares my admiration for
the Native Americans, and to those
among them who are striving to renew
their cultural heritage and spiritual
strength that mankind may come into
harmony with earth and sky.

Contents

Foreword   *x*

Introduction   *xii*

Map   *xvi*

Map key   *xvii*

Glossary   *xix*

List of months   *xxii*

1   He who was of the old ones   1

2   He who learns wisdom   9

3   Out of the east comes danger   27

4   The meaning of a vision   34

5   Early war trails   47

6   Storm clouds from the east   60

7   Little wars and bad luck   78

8   The great vision   100

9   It is hard to hold to a great vision   115

10 The last war cry   133

11 The old songs shall die for awhile   148

12 The Crazy Horse monument   165

Foreword

Because such an Indian as Crazy Horse should have lived to leave his moccasin prints upon the sands of time—with honor and credibility—because from these particles of earth in their minuteness there should rise in monumental grandeur an entire sculptured mountain depicting the greatness of the Oglala warrior and holy man, I humbly undertake this task as a Lakota (Sioux) of today to salute another Lakota brother of yesterday. For it was his ancestors and mine who, in the beginning, sat encircled as blood brothers, each beside the fire of his tribe in grand assemblage—to become known as the "Council of Seven Fires." From this circle of oneness in brotherhood sprang the great Lakota Nation. From this primeval setting came the wisdom and accord that seemed to blaze anew with each lighting of the "Seven Fires." And the fires burned fiercely and unabatingly through the unfettered centuries before the "white wings" appeared on the crest of the Atlantic. And when the tortured years of submission dogged the retreating Indian, and courageous Indian leaders were subjected to often inhuman physical trials, there was born among the Oglala tribe a boy of unusual sensitivity and awareness who exploded into an adulthood of spirituality equaling the greatest of our spiritualists and religionists. That his fire should spurt forth with renewed brightness and avowed dedication to a cause—of a very existence—shedding its light among the shadows of doom, first for a defeated people, and now for all of mankind—perhaps caused a well-intentioned author to seek to bring to the world a message of new awareness. Feathered with his own awareness as a man of Nature, the author has selected a man of historic proportion whose stature may be of a magnitude that might strike home to mankind the impact of ecology and its manifestations before it is too late.

I am in agreement with the author in his selection of this notable figure in American history, Chief Crazy Horse, whose greatness is being inscribed today on the face of a mountain in South Dakota and whose countenance will forever be "Great upon the Mountain," the sacred Black Hills of his honored homeland.

This writing, in its newness and the contemporary concepts of the author, may be that "light in the forest" which so many of our children, youth, and people in general seek in an ever-expanding quest for the great mysteries of our Native Americans.

> Red Dawn—Santee Sioux
> Stephen S. Jones, Jr. (*English name*)

Introduction

The Little Waves and the Big Wave

Why am I writing this book, I who was an atheist for many years, overproud of my objective scientific approach, and for whom the meaning of the Spirit was only a fairy story told by childish men? I do not know fully, though I see gleamings. A strong light came when I stood on the top of Bear Butte, the Sacred Mountain of both the Cheyennes and the Lakota (Sioux) of the northern Great Plains. It was dark that night and a cold wind whispered and howled out of the west, blowing through the flimsy blanket that was my only protection, forcing me sometimes to shiver even though my eyes were seeing the glory of a sky filled with stars like rivers of misty light and I was throwing my prayers to the Daybreak Star in the east with all my might.

A holy man of the Oglala Lakota had brought me and two others to that Sacred Mountain, making the ceremony for a Hanblecheyapi, the vision quest of the plains tribes, and teaching us the details as to how we should pray and cry for our vision to the Lord of All That Is. Now we stood on the very top of this mountain, with lights above us and light below, yet sheathed in thick darkness, together and yet alone as if we were on separate stars. Each of us was surrounded by the four colors of the four directions, black to the west, red to the north, yellow to the east and white to the south, but we were also surrounded by the whole circle of earth and sky and the greater circle of the universe. To the sacred four directions we sent our prayers and also up to Father Sky twice—one for the Great Spirit and one for the soul of man. Then our prayers were sent down to Mother Earth, and so to the Seven Powers of the Universe, representing the Great Spirit. Day and night the rhythm of these song prayers was to be thrown out from the heart, until a vision came.

I saw the dawn coming, glow by glow, light by growing light, dark gray and light gray, gray-yellow and yellow, yellow and gold, red with the eternal fire when finally the red disk of the sun shone through the light clouds that lined the eastern horizon. And then the glory burst in a red flame around the circle of the horizon and over the earth and down onto the plains, even into the valleys and the canyons, and the greening earth was below us, far below, in its majesty and beauty, the plains like emerald waves running to the four directions and southwest to the Black Hills, *Paha Sapa*, dark green and majestic like a great bear, humped and double-humped and peaked like huge ears. *Now I saw the circle, the great circle of all that is, all life and all human life, that must dwell and walk in beauty. Never, I knew, could we human beings rest until all men awoke out of their sleep, pierced the darkness to the light, and made first their hearts and then the whole earth beautiful again.*

Crazy Horse too had sought a vision on Bear Butte. He too had seen and known the beauty and power of the sacred circle, the reality behind all things. He had fought as only a great hero can fight to save his people and keep them in that circle, but he had seen them go down and down into darkness like a stricken ship sinking in a terrible storm, down and down through whirlpools of the sickness being introduced into their circle by another people.

But it was the people of the little waves that went down, those who saw only their own time and mistook its dark things for light; not him, for he was a great wave that saw beyond the far horizons to the day when the eternal wheel of time would turn once more, even as the earth turns on its axis to meet again the sun, and a glory and greatness would come. He gives to all of us a light and a hope and, in writing this book, I pass that hope and light on to you.

This is a story, then, of the life of Crazy Horse, but it is not a biography that deals in details and what men call facts, but that are sometimes only the shadows of much greater things and truths. This is a book of a spiritual adventure, my adventure, and yours too if you can follow me on a trail that sometimes leads through the mists and the shadows of the valleys and sometimes leads us to the clearness and sharpness of the peaks. Though I follow the main outline of what others have written about Crazy Horse, I leave their earth-bound tracks for the sky at times, for a voice comes to me with a whisper in the dawn when I am half-awake and sings of things of the spirit that no man can tie with earth-bound thongs. So you can say to yourself, if you wish, this is largely fiction dreamed by a human mind, and read the story just for the enjoyment it will give you, or perhaps you can reach beyond such limitations and see that soul can touch soul down the long sun-pierced but shadow-darkened trail of man, and some realities and truths bigger than any of us can emerge out of such touching.

And why again do I write such a book, I who am and have been so weak and frail a human being, who have done such foolish things, who have so often faltered on the trail and dipped backwards into darkness? I write because I believe the Lord of the Trackless Skies watches our falls with sorrow and anger, but cheers us on with joy and spirit when we rise again and struggle upward toward the light, when we glimpse that far-off gleam of something greater than men have ever dreamed of, and fight to bring with us all mankind into the love and understanding that will make the glorious sunlight of a new day of honor and of greatness.

Vinson Brown

Map of major events in the life of Crazy Horse

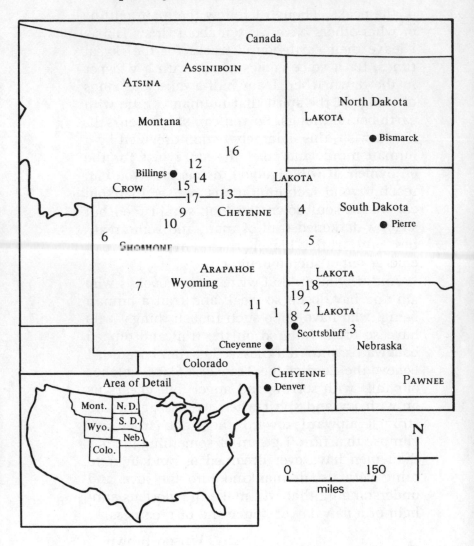

This map shows the country of the Teton Lakota (earliest Sioux to live on the Plains), and some of the neighboring tribes.

"My land is where my dead lie buried!"

(Key to the numbers shown on the map.)

1. Curly sees Conquering Bear, chief of the Oglala Lakota, wounded near old Fort Laramie because of the madness of the whites, 1854.
2. Curly watches Conquering Bear die and near this point seeks a vision.
3. Curly finds women and children killed at a Brulé Camp on the Blue Water, which was attacked by a soldier column under Harney, 1855.
4. Bear Butte, the sacred mountain, where the Teton Lakota have their Great Council in the summer of 1856, and where Crazy Horse has a great vision.
5. Rapid Creek, along which Curly was born, and where he discusses his first vision with his father in the fall of 1857.
6. Oglala war party, with young Curly along, makes raid far to the west, and Curly kills some enemies in battle.
7. Young Crazy Horse is in battle with Shoshones in the valley of Sweetwater where the son of Chief Washakie is killed by the Lakota, June 20, 1861.
8. Free Lakotas help captured ones escape at Horse Creek, 1865.
9. Battle of the Hundred Slain. Fetterman's column decoyed to their deaths by Crazy Horse and others, December 21, 1866.

10.   Many-shooting guns at Wagon-box Fight hold off Indians, 1867.

11.   Crazy Horse and war party attack Horse-shoe Station, March 1868.

12. He Dog and Crazy Horse lead successful war party against Crows.

13.   Camp of Two Moons and He Dog attacked by Reynolds, March 17, 1876. Starving and half-frozen people flee to camp of Crazy Horse.

14.   Battle of the Rosebud. Crook driven back by Indian allies, led by Crazy Horse, Gall, and others, June 17, 1876.

15.   Battle of the Little Bighorn, June 25, 1876.

16.   Lakota peace chiefs killed at Fort Keogh by Crow scouts, December 1876.

17.   General Miles attacks Crazy Horse's camp, January 8, 1877.

18.   Crazy Horse takes wife to Spotted Tail, September 4, 1877.

19.   At Fort Robinson Crazy Horse is killed, September 5, 1877.

Glossary

(Note: Lakota, in original form, put the main word before the descriptive words. Example: Wichasha Wakan; Man Holy.)

Akicita: Persons chosen by a Lakota council to work among the warriors in a disciplinary way, making sure the best interests of the people were served.

Hanblcchcyapi: Crying for a vision. Facing manhood, a young Lakota often went alone to ask for a vision of what was asked of his life. This sacred quest was also made by older ones and by women.

Hoka Hey; Hoye: Cries used in battle by warriors defending their villages with courage.

Hou: Greetings.

Inipi: Sacred purification ceremony conducted by a Wichasha Wakan (Holy Man), taking place in a sweat lodge to purify the Lakota man or woman for a sacred vision quest.

Itanca: One who has assumed the responsibility for his circle of people, and therefore thinks first of them, protecting them against enemies and finding hunting grounds that provide food and shelter (meat and skins), and is devoted to maintaining unity within the camp circle of his people.

Kola: Friend.

Lakota: Originally "Lakota" meant "The Friendly People" (of the Seven Council Fires). The Council Fire into which Crazy Horse was born was the Teton. Other Council Fires of the seven used the word "Dakota." The other six Council Fires were Yankton, Yanktonais, Mdewakantonwan, Wahpekute, Wahpton, Sisseton. The Teton (a word meaning village or dwellers on the plain) Council Fire grew and in time was made up of the Sicangu (Burnt Thigh), or Brule (a French name), Minneconjou (Planting near the Water), Hunkpapa (Campers at the Horn, or End), Itazipco (No Bows), Sihasapa (Blackfeet), Oohenumpa (Two Kettles) and Oglala. Oglala, meaning "to pour something powdery," was the circle into which Crazy Horse was born, and his father before him. Sicangu, or in French, Brule, was the circle from which his mother came when she married into the Oglalas. The Oglalas, in time growing larger, had become bands based largely on family ties and traveling in numbers suitable to the life of moving quickly with the game they hunted. Hunkpatila is the band to which Crazy Horse belonged.

The traditional Lakota still term themselves Lakota. Sioux is not a Lakota word.

It is a gallicized version of the ending of the Chippewa word "Nadowessi" (snake) which the Chippewa called the Lakota and Dakota in respect for their quickly learned fighting skill as the fight for land began with tribes pushed against tribes by the white onrushing settlers. French trappers and traders in that area of the Chippewa-Lakota clash, the headwaters of the Mississippi, added the French plural to the Chippewa word, making it Nadowessioux, and later the word was shortened.

Matohoshila: Bear Boy.

Minne-wakan: Minne—Water; *wakan*—Spirit or Holy. The Lakota first called the effects of alcohol strange and mysterious, as if holy or spirit. They later saw the bad results it left in its path and the leaders made great efforts to keep their reservation lands assigned far from the river ports and other sources of alcohol.

Paha Mata: Paha—Hill or Butte; *Mata*—Bear. Bear Butte was the setting of the Hanble-cheyapi of Crazy Horse.

Paha Sapa: Paha—Hill; *Sapa*—Black. The Black Hills were sacred to the Lakota and they would only enter them when seriously seeking guidance.

Wakan Tanka: Wakan—Holy or Spirit; *Tanka*—Great.

Wagichun: Wagi—Talking; *chun*—Tree. The sacred tree of the Lakota is the Cottonwood Tree or Talking Tree, because of the noise its leaves make in a wind.

Waglukhe: Loafers about the Forts. Those

Lakota who went in earlier to receive fort
and then reservation supplies, thus giving
up the independent hunting life, were
called this by the Lakota who, along with
Crazy Horse and Sitting Bull and similar
leaders, maintained the independent life as
long as possible.

Wasichus: Whites.

Wichasha Wakan: Wichasha—man; *Wakan*—
Holy or Spirit or Medicine.

Yuipi: Sacred ceremony of healing and guidance, conducted by the Wichasha Wakan
(Holy Man).

*Throughout the book the months will be
referred to by the Lakota words.*

January—Moon of Frosting in the Lodge
February—Moon of the Dark Red Calves
March—Moon of Snow Blindness
April—Moon of Tender Grass (or New Grass)
May—Moon of Ponies Shedding Hair
June—Moon of Making Fat
July—Moon of Cherries Reddening
August—Moon of Cherries Black
September—Moon of Calves Growing
            Black Hair
October—Moon of Colored Leaves
November—Moon of Falling Leaves
December—Moon of Popping Trees (in frost)

Chapter 1

He who was of the old ones

From the peaks of the Paha Sapa, the Sacred Black Hills of the Lakota, the Sioux, the wind sings through the dark needles of the pines, chanting a song about the Strange Man of the Oglala, Crazy Horse, holy man and warrior. It sings of a man big as the sacred circle of the blue sky and the brown earth, bigger than the Oglala, the Hunkpapa, the Brulé, and all the other divisions of the Lakota, bigger than the Wasichus, the white people, who wished his death, big enough to bring a message to awaken all peoples.

It is not without meaning that they carve his feather and his face, his body and his horse, on the great white stone of Paha Sapa, the granite of the hills, heart of the earth, old as time. It is no wonder they shall carve him bigger than the four heads of the presidents at Mount Rushmore, bigger than Washington and Jefferson,

1

Lincoln and Theodore Roosevelt, the greatest of the Great Fathers who ruled America. Crazy Horse knew a courage as wonderful as the courage of Washington in the dark days of Valley Forge; he knew a message as great as the message of Jefferson in the Declaration of Independence; he knew a wisdom as fine as the wisdom of Lincoln in the Second Inaugural; and he knew also a teaching of the earth and its life greater than that of Theodore Roosevelt, who trumpeted the call for conservation to a sleeping America.

Out of the earth and the wilderness, the gurgle of the waters, the pungent scent of the sagebrush, the scream of the eagle, the thunder of buffaloes, the voice of Crazy Horse still calls to us. Though he died in a time of darkness, held by some of his own people so he might be killed by sharp steel in his back, as foretold in his great vision, though the Sioux and all the Indians were sinking swiftly into the shadows, closing in from every direction, into the stink of corruption, the poisonous forgetfulness of alcohol, the web of lies made by the two-tongued and the dark of mind, he left us a legend that shall be deathless. From his death and his people's death of spirit, his own people, the Native Americans, shall rise like the Phoenix, the Thunder Bird, to a glory immeasurable, and they shall teach other people how to find that glory. It is meet; it is just that the least shall become the most, even as the Bible foretells, and as is symbolized by the great figure of Crazy Horse rising in long carvings on the vast granite of the Paha Sapa,* the symbol of the original inhabitants of America, coming back to greatness.

One, two, three, four, almost five centuries of dishonor have come to the red men of America, from the time of Columbus, from the sacking of Tenochtitlan, most beautiful of cities, from the days of the Pilgrim fathers and the padres of California, from the Trail of Tears of the Cherokees, Choctaws, and Creeks, from the defeat of Tecumseh, bitter as ashes, and the broken heart of Chief Joseph, knowing his children were lost and starving. But the days of injustice and misunderstanding must end. Out of suffering beyond suffering the red people shall rise again and it shall be a blessing for a sick world, a world weary of blindness and darkness, selfishness and separations, and longing for the light.

The true wonder and glory of Crazy Horse is not that he possibly killed more of the white invaders than any other Indian, not that he sometimes stood alone in the councils of the chiefs speaking for justice, not that no bullet in countless battles was capable of hitting him, not that he was the greatest leader, as some say, in the defeats of generals Crook and Custer at the battles of the Rosebud and the Little Bighorn. These were all signs of great courage and sensitivity of a leader, willing to live and die for his people, as "Itanca" must do. His people take rightful pride in these parts of his life.

* The Crazy Horse Monument near Custer, South Dakota, in the Black Hills.

Still these were all as shadows in the fire-light, the dying dust of an old buffalo trail, compared to his true glory. His greatness lay in the purity to which he raised his life, beyond pride and vanity, and his knowledge of the true reality that lies behind the empty face of human power and wealth and desire. Out of the Silence he drew his strength and out of that Silence, in whose harmony he lived, he joins the ranks of the deathless heroes of history to teach us the meaning of a greatness all of us need, even more than the thirsty in the desert are desperate for water.

Crazy Horse knew that all the shame and shoddiness, the lies and the power-grabbing that came with the conquest of his people were not of the great circle of life and the universe. The Roundness, the Indians of many tribes called that circle in the old days, a Roundness that meant the singing of the mother to her baby under the whispering cottonwoods, lullabies of love and hope, or the deeper chanting of the old ones to the youth, telling the legends, the great tales of heroism and purity and courage, or the kindness of the camp circle where all were good neighbors and worked together in triumph or disaster, while the young, strong hunters brought the rumps and the tongues— the best meat of the buffaloes—to the widows and the old people, to the sick and the orphans.

But it is a Roundness also of all mankind, the Holy Ones understood. It encompasses the standards the Great Spirit has always set for their lives, standards of honor and purity, kindness and courage and strength of soul, which lead them out of the shadows even as the sun takes us out of the night into glorious light.

As a child Crazy Horse sat in the magic circle of the campfire, seeing strange figures dancing in the flames and hearing the wind talking among the leaves of the Wagichun, the sacred cottonwood tree. He loved to hear an old holy man of his people, a Wichasha Wakan, tell the marvelous story of the White Buffalo Calf Maiden, the Sacred Being, who brought the seven sacred ceremonies and the seven sacred circles of the sacred pipe to the Lakota. Can you see that boy listening? He listened with his whole mind and his whole soul, not as do the wanderers, the lost Indians of this generation, those whose ears have been closed by the white men and who have been driven to wander in darkness, though crying in their hearts for the knowledge they need so badly.

Centuries of deceit and brainwashing have brought them to this state, but many now are seeking for the lost secrets and are beginning to find them again.

So Crazy Horse knew deeply that story—how two young men went forth to hunt and stood on a high hill watching for game, but saw instead a maiden coming across the plain toward them. When she drew near they saw that she was clothed in handsome buckskin, covered with quilled designs, and that she carried a bundle covered with buckskin under one arm. Now one of them saw that she was very young and very beautiful and his passion was strong with desire for her so that he spoke his thoughts. But the other hunter said, "Put away such bad thoughts, for she is a sacred woman."

Her feet moved like the butterflies as she walked across the grasslands; her hair waved in the breeze like the silk of corn; her eyes glowed as does the sky at sunrise. "Come over to me!" she called to the one whose thoughts were uncontrolled and her voice was as singing waters. "Come!" she called, "and you shall have what you want!"

The one with the immature thoughts ran eagerly and a cloud descended upon him and the sacred maiden so that they were hidden. When the cloud rose, the girl still stood there, but the young and foolish man was only a skeleton lying on the ground being eaten by worms! Then the sacred one told the man whose heart was good and strong to go back to his people and have them prepare a great lodge for her since she would come to give them an important message.

Can you see that boy, who was to be Crazy Horse, listening to that story? In his heart he understood that the maiden was telling him that all women and girls bear within them the great mystery of life's beginning, which the Great Spirit wishes to be nurtured with love inside a family that is filled with love, and not to be touched by the immature of heart who seek only for pleasure. So Crazy Horse saw then that all women were sacred beings and he vowed in his soul that he would be like that good man.

But he listened also to the rest of that story of the White Buffalo Calf Maiden, and how she came to his people, walking in a sacred manner,

and told them of the Sacred Circle of their oneness and love, and how they would smoke the
Sacred Pipe she gave to them, and use it in
Seven Sacred Ceremonies that would purify
them and make them good and honorable to
all men and women, protectors of all children,
and lovers of the Great Spirit. So the young
boy, who was to become Crazy Horse, took these
things into his soul until they were like part of
his bone and blood. Increasingly Crazy Horse
worked to speak the straight tongue that speaks
only the truth, knowing that the Great Spirit
sees into all hearts and asks of all men the
beauty in thoughts and words of crystal clear
waters. He grew more and more humble, knowing how little he was and how much he had to
learn, feeling the Earth beneath his feet, the
Earth Mother, knowing she nurtured all life
and was greater than he and yet allowed him
to walk on her body. He became one who was
too honorable to speak ill of other men; it being
more important to see the vision of what they,
and the earth, are to become. Even though he
sometimes faltered on the trail, as nearly all
human beings do, he always returned to the
circle. A man need not be perfect to be a great
man, but he must learn from all his experi-
ences, good and bad, and develop beyond them
through thought, prayer, and action, or his
greatness will only be dust upon the wind. *And
so must we all, for the time has come for men
to grow up and become true men, putting aside
lies and backbiting, immature use of each other
and Mother Earth, else the whole world dies!
The earth hangs on the brink of a war that*

*would destroy all that lives, and only the hearts
that become pure and strong can save it.*

Let us listen then, to the whisper sung by the
wind through the sacred pines in the Paha Sapa,
the Black Hills, telling the story of Crazy Horse,
holy man and warrior. Let us listen, for he sets
the example to the Indians first and then to all
people of a life to live of courage and honor,
and we need this song and this story, as a man
hanging helpless on the edge of a great cliff
needs the strong hand of rescue! Listen then
and be quiet, for this is a song out of the Stillness, and the Stillness is Wakan Tanka, and
Wakan Tanka is the Spirit of all that is sacred
in the whole universe. Hear now the hills talking to you, the grass waving like golden curtains
under the wind, the four-leggeds leaping over
the earth and the winged ones skimming
through the blue. All things beautiful and good
are calling to you, for the two-leggeds, white
man and red, yellow man and black alike, have
killed too much of life, and made the earth ugly
with smog and trash and pollution, wars and
quarrels and lies, until it is time indeed to make
our hearts and the whole world beautiful again.

Chapter 2

He who learns wisdom

Now the boy who was to become Crazy Horse was first called Curly because of his curling hair of brown, and some Indians foolishly spoke ill of him because he was paler of skin than most of them. But his father was a holy man of the Lakota, a Wichasha Wakan, who had the old and honorable name of Crazy Horse, and his father told him wisely not to worry, that a man stood in the eyes of Wakan Tanka, the Great Spirit, by his goodness of heart, his courage, and his deeds, untouched by the talk of the foolish ones. And Curly remembered this, and, when he became older, judged not all white men by their skin color, but found among them some few who he knew were brave and good and honorable.

This was not common to find, however. For the troops and treaty commissioners and agents sent for Western duty were not typically the honorable segment of white society. Especially was this true in a time when the Civil War was drawing off officers and troops, leaving ruffians for Western duty. The pay and working conditions offered agents and treaty commissioners did not draw the conscientious and honorable, but rather the opposite. Still today the people of Crazy Horse understandably judge the non-Indian by the examples of these people, and their picture is a grim one.

When a boy, Crazy Horse learned to leap on the backs of the half-wild horses of the Lakota and tear whooping across the plains. He knew himself to be a member of the Oglala people, though he knew also his blood had in it other divisions of the Lakota, such as the Brulé and Minneconjou, and even some Shyela, as the Lakota called their allies, the Cheyennes.

He practiced with the bow and arrow and hunted with other boys for jackrabbits and prairie dogs and grouse until his shots almost always hit the mark. In youth he grew strong enough to run far on the hills and chase down a wounded antelope or deer as does the great wolf of the plains. And when he killed, he chanted a prayer that the Indians of old always sang over the four-leggeds and the winged ones at death, for they too are part of the Great Circle of Life, the Children of the Great Spirit, and one does not take their life lightly or without humility.

It was Hump, the great warrior and good man, who became the chief teacher or warrior father of young Curly, for each boy of the people must have such a man to follow and learn from. But Curly was lucky above other boys, for

Hump had the wisdom of the earth within him and the courage of the grizzly bear and the buffalo bull and the skill in hunting and fighting of one who has long followed the trail of man and animal and learned from everyone a good lesson. Like his father, Curly knew Hump had always used the straight tongue and spoke no evil about other men in the camp, but was silent unless he could say something good.

So Curly went with Hump on the hunting trail and the war trail. He saw this man waste no movement nor any word, but hold the bow or the lance or the gun steady as a rock and strike when the striking counted. He learned from Hump how to lie still for hours, waiting for game, to find the sign of the deer or bear in the slight bending of the grass, to make the clever snares of sedge reed or willow bark for the rabbits and a thousand other tricks of the wild. What glory he felt in racing the antelope, leaping in yellow and black waves over the hills of the Greasy Grass, the Little Bighorn, where the smell of danger hung in the air from the enemy camps of the Crows. He hunted the buffalo in the shallows of the Tongue River with his cousins, the Shyelas (Cheyennes), and put his arrow in behind the hump of a big black bull when it splashed through the waters, staggering onto the farther bank and dying with mouth gushing crimson blood on the white sands.

Glorious were the days of spring and summer and fall on the wild plains at the hunting, with the grass hip-high beneath his running horse; juicy and rich the buffalo humps and tongues, cooked over the fire at twilight; wonderful the singing when the drums beat and the night wind called among the tipis, and the women trilled their praise at the accounts of the hunters and warriors.

But there was pain among the joy in the circle of the Lakota. The horizon was closing in, less land and food, tribes fighting for the little remaining. And so young Curly listened gravely when the tales came of both Brulés and Oglalas down at the traders' stations drinking of the fiery liquid that made men crazy so that some of the young and foolish fought and wounded or killed each other over petty things like a blanket or a beaded bag. And, when he went to the fort of the Wasichus, the white men, at Laramie, he saw with his own eyes the drinking from the dark bottles and the faces turning stupid or wild, the staggering of those who looked as though struck in the head, and the flaming of tempers that brought forth the violence of knife or hatchet or gun.

"Ho!" growled Hump, "the Wasichus have driven our people mad with this drink! They have forgotten the red road [of goodness] and the circle of the Roundness. To hide their shame they learn to speak with the two tongues!" And young Curly nodded his head in agreement, for he was slow to use his voice, but he swore in his heart that he would never touch such a foolish drink.

But it was on the outskirts of Fort Laramie, where the drinking and drunkenness had been so bad, that Curly had a strange adventure that helped him later to see with the eyes of the

Great Spirit. The Hunkpatila band of the Oglala Lakota, of which Curly and his family were members, had camped for some weeks of trading near the fort to wait for the annual gratuity of blankets and guns and powder that the white men brought from the one they called the Great Father, the President of the United States. Hump, as usual, had growled over this foolishness, which he said was merely a way to lure the people away from the life of goodness and freedom under the Sacred Tree of their religion. But Red Cloud and others of the warriors, including even Conquering Bear, head leader of the Oglala, brought the people here because they said the Lakota had to learn and understand the white man's way. And after all, were not these things given to them as their right because the white men used a road (called the "holy road" because it was to be left alone) across the Indian country?

"Yes," growled Hump again, "but wait till the first road grows forks like a cottonwood sapling and spreads into a tree of roads that fills all the Indians' lands. What then?" But few wished to listen to him, dreaming of the bright beads and blankets and other good things the white men would bring.

One day Curly went off alone to straighten and feather his arrows and to do some thinking and dreaming about a certain Black Buffalo Girl whose face had turned crimson when he looked at her. He was so deep in his dreams that his usual Indian alertness failed him, and he looked up suddenly to see a white-skinned, fair-haired boy standing on a little knoll covered with buffalo grass fifty feet away, watching him intently. He was on his feet in an instant, wildly thinking, How did he get so near without my hearing him? In the next second he had an arrow fitted to his bow and the string drawn back, but the white boy, who was about thirteen like himself, raised both hands empty to show he had no weapons, and greeted him in Lakota:

"*Hou, Kola!*"

"*Hou, Kola!*" answered Curly, and lowered his bow.

The white boy smiled a good clear smile and spoke again in the language of the people. "My mother is one of you," he said, as if to explain his talking the language.

"But your skin is so white."

The white boy flushed. "She is the only mother I know, though I had one long ago who had the same skin color as I have. But because I love so much this mother I have now, I wish to be a Lakota. Can you help me?"

His voice was so sincere that Curly could not help smiling. He beckoned so the white boy came near and sat down beside him. The two looked at each other for a long time without words spoken. Curly was pleased to see that he did not chatter as too many whites did, but had already learned something of the Indian way of talking silently with the spirit.

"Wait for me here," said Curly at last, "till the sun is almost setting, and I will bring some things to make you be like an Indian."

The boy nodded his head and prepared himself silently.

When Curly came back, he brought with him a bowl and some plants that his mother had given him, she who always knew what this strange son of her sister, now her son, needed, often without even being asked. He started a little fire, got water from a spring, and soon was boiling the plants in it. A while later, when this mixture had cooled into a brown paste, he began rubbing the white boy's skin and hair with it, until they turned a dark brown from the dye, and the fair-skinned boy was no more. Then they looked at each other and laughed a secret laughter that suddenly made everything good between them.

"I will call you by a good name—Matohoshila [Bear Boy]," said Curly. "Come tomorrow, just before the sun rises, and I will take you to my family. We will teach you truly to be a Lakota."

Bear Boy nodded his head in his silent, understanding way, and disappeared over the knoll.

When they met in the morning, Curly taught him the Dawn Song that the Indian sings to the rising sun, the song that lifts up to the sky like the song of the meadowlark and has the same joy and wonder in it; the song that tells how the earth and sky are all part of one big circle, with the Great Spirit in the center, and man learning to be part of it.

After a bit of practice, the two boys sang the song together, even though usually it is supposed to be sung alone, but the two felt now as if they were one being. So the song rose on the sweet wild air of the Great Plains, up and up to the clear blue of the sky and around the horizon where the flame of the sunrise was ringing. It came from their hearts and from their souls and because it did, they felt they were part of the distant clouds to the west, part of the white-throated swifts who were darting high above across the sky like winged arrows, part of the soft brown earth and the green grass, and part of a distant group of antelope whose feet seemed scarcely to touch the ground as they bounded across the great plain. And they knew, in the way of all those whose spirits truly touch the wild, that the Silent One was in them and above them and around them.

They went to their horses, sprang onto their backs, and in that same companionable holy silence rode to the tipi of Crazy Horse, the father of Curly. Here, when they smelled the good smell of cooking buffalo meat and greens, they became boys again, eager for the food, and wolfishly chewing it while they grinned at each other happily. Curly's mother and father watched them with pleasure, noting that the new boy thanked them politely for the food and bowed his head in silent prayer before the first bite.

But the reception from Hump was different. He stared at Bear Boy a long time, then reached forward and felt his hair.

"This is a Wasichu," he growled.

"He is my friend!" Curly cried. "He wants to be a Lakota because his foster mother is Lakota and he likes our ways. I have darkened his skin to make him like us, and already he speaks our tongue."

"He is still a Wasichu. You can change the

color of the skin, but you cannot change the inside."

Curly's mother stood up. Her eyes spoke to her husband. "May I speak?" they asked him. The father nodded his head and she became straight, like a tall pine, her eyes beginning to mist over with the look of a dreamer.

She said to Hump, "I have learned much from the far-seeing ones. The white people are outside the Sacred Circle, because they have lost touch with the Great Spirit. They are sick in their hearts and this is why they do so many crazy things, killing without meaning, and using lies when they foolishly think it helps them. They are hurting our people and they will continue to hurt them. But they know nothing of the Sacred Way; even their priests only know it partly, because they blind themselves behind little walls of differences. Yet this will not always be so. They were made by the Great Spirit, just as we were made by Him. They too are part of the circle of life, even though they do not understand. Someday the Great Spirit will bring them into the Sacred Circle, and there are some few already, like this boy, whose eyes are open and who are seeking. I have seen in my dreams the day when there will be a great many like him, and they will come to our people in thousands and thousands asking for help. Our people too, in those days, will be outside the Circle because they will have lost themselves in the storms the white people bring and they will have only the memory of the good days when all of us were under the wings of the Above One. Then our people too will begin to awaken and come into a great circle of unity, gathering their strength like the Thunders coming out of the west. That will be a glorious day. But remember always that the Wasichus too are the children of the Great Spirit. They are lost, but one day He will lead them again out of darkness into light! And one day we will all be brothers, like this one and our son."

She sat down and was silent again, her eyes looking to the ground, and the others saw only the good wife, quiet and shy, and they were amazed at what she had spoken.

Hump gave the signal to Curly and Bear Boy and the two youths followed him out to the horses. When they were mounted, he turned to Bear Boy. "The woman may be right," he admitted. "I believe she sees what I cannot see, and I know she walks the sacred way. We will test you to see if you understand and if you too can walk the path where the Thunders lead."

Bear Boy rode erect on his horse like a warrior and was silent, but his eyes eloquently told them he would follow their way.

Two hours later they dismounted on the top of a high butte overlooking the plains below, and Hump led them to the highest rock of all, where they could see the great circle of the horizon on all sides. He swept his arm around the circle, then drew his long pipe from the sacred bag that he had brought, and sent smoke curling to the four directions, then twice up to Father Sky and once down to Mother Earth. When the circle of the ceremony was complete, and he had sung a song to the Silence, he sheathed the pipe once more in its bag and turned to Bear Boy.

"Here is peace," he said, "in the center of the Universe, which is our circle. Remember this peace when you are in battle, when you are hunting, always remember it in times of danger particularly, but in all times. Live up to this peace of the Spirit and do harm to no one without just cause. Be kind to the weak, the children and women, be kind to all men and to all living things, killing only when you need food or clothing, or to protect the weak ones, but killing quickly so you do not cause pain. If you see a girl or a woman alone, do her no harm, nor have any bad thoughts about her, but protect her, for she is a sacred being, and this is the teaching of the Above One. Women are sacred because they are givers of life and their purpose is to raise that life in harmony with all creation in a happy family protected by love where the wife is sensitive to the husband, and both husband and wife are faithful to each other so that no jealousy or quarreling or hidden secrets shall rise in that family, poisoning the air and making the children restless and disturbed and unhappy because there is something wrong between their parents. Out of such sick families come the sick ones who cause trouble between men.

"Sing the songs of the Sacred Circle every day, in the dawn, at midday, and in the nighttime, but other times also, especially when there is a great job to be done or when there is danger, or when you feel wrong toward another person, so that quickly you may feel right. When you sing the songs and are in the circle, you cannot tell a lie any more than you would take a knife and cut out your own tongue. You cannot hurt others because you know the Great Spirit leads you only in the straight way of kindness and honor. Make this a habit, day after day without fail all the days of your life. If you ever weaken and fall outside the circle, it is still possible to come back if you climb to the hill or mountaintop and cry with all your heart to the Great Spirit, telling him you have been wrong and asking forgiveness, but he will not help you unless your heart and words are sincere. And do not blame other men or women and make bad words against them, for none can judge others, only the Great Spirit who knows all things and sees into every heart and mind.

"And when you go to choose a wife, do not be in a hurry, but be patient and watch her for a long time to make sure she is right for you, and listen to your elders who may know her, telling the difference between those who speak about her with envy or ill feeling from those who speak about her with wisdom, for the latter will be kind even though they may warn you and in their voices you will hear their sincerity. Remember she must live to be strong when you are weak with sickness or are wounded in battle, and come to your aid in all times of difficulty, not being a fair-weather wife, even as you must be strong also in the Great Spirit. So also must she be loyal to you. And so test her loyalty and her love before you marry her, not afterward when it is too late. Then will the two of you form a nest, like the nest of the quail, and in the circle of that nest you will rear beautiful children who call on the Great Spirit by name day and night and walk the sacred way of goodness to all men."

Hump had been talking quietly, but now he turned and looked into the eyes of Bear Boy. He looked for a long time.

"Do you understand?" he asked at last. When the boy looked back seriously and nodded his head, Hump reached out his hand and touched the skin over the heart. "It is good," he said. "Here is where the boy decides to be a man, and today I see you have decided. May you always follow the path where the Thunders lead, the straight path and the straight tongue of the Great Spirit."

The boy was silent for a while and so were the other two, looking around the circle of earth and sky, seeing the green grass of the plains in waves stretching to the edge of the earth, and hearing the swallows crying as they circled the bluff, catching insects. Far below a bob-o-link called his crystal song, and they felt the presence of the Silent One.

Then Bear Boy asked: "What more must I do?"

"We will show you many things," said Hump. "How to follow a trail in darkness or in light; how to stand pain without murmuring; how to ride many hours without tiring; how to help others in trouble; how to hunt and how to fight when it is necessary to protect the helpless ones; how to feel and see like a mountain lion, so you sense everything around you, even without hearing or seeing; how to send your spirit out like the eagle when he climbs toward the sun, never pulling it inward in fear or worry.

"When you are trained in all these things, we will make the Inipi purification ceremony with the sweat bath, and then the Hanblecheyapi ceremony to prepare you for crying for a vision. To a sacred place on the mountain we will send you to seek for a vision. And then you will hope to find your sacred name and be strong as a warrior and a man so that the Great Spirit will speak to you through a four legged one, or a winged one, or even from the mouths of the Thunder Beings, or out of the Rainbow. For to each man who seeks with a pure heart He comes in a different way, but those who are not pure shall have nothing."

And the boy was silent for a while as the wise youth learns to be, thinking of all these things Hump had said. Then he drew himself tall and straight, and said simply: "I am ready to do what you want."

Curly and Bear Boy stood together after that in the tests that Hump gave them, trying to run faster and farther, to ride like the wind, to follow the tracks of the animals, to watch in silence from behind a bush or rock the secret ways of the wild, and to harden their muscles in all the ways of the Indian. And so a month passed swiftly, and between the two was a brotherhood that would be remembered always. And then came disaster!

It all happened because of a foolish white man and a foolish cow. The cow, being driven

by a white man of one of the wagon trains, had
run away from its master, and broke into the
Lakota camp, knocking over pots and pans,
breaking lodges, raising a rumpus until a young
Minneconjou Lakota warrior shot it dead and
then butchered it so the meat would pay for all
the damage it had done. But the white man
went on to the military at Fort Laramie and
complained bitterly that the Indians had killed
his cow and demanded they be punished. It
would have been passed over with little inci-
dent, and a horse given the white man to pay
for his cow, if he had not kept demanding
punishment for the culprit, and if an equally
foolish young lieutenant named Grattan had not
taken up the cry for punishment and offered to
lead a group of soldiers to get the man who
killed the cow.

Lieutenant Grattan took thirty soldiers and
two wagon guns, whose shots could kill several
Indians at once, and went to the Sioux camp to
arrest young Straight Foretop, the Minneconjou who had killed the cow. The foolish Grattan, egged on by a still more foolish and partly
drunken half-breed interpreter named Wyuse,
made such outrageous demands that the
Lakota became angry too, and the words
turned into the firing of a gun by a soldier so
that a great storm broke loose as the warriors
came swarming over the river bank, Grattan
falling from a bullet from Straight Foretop, and
Conquering Bear crashing down with a half-
dozen bad wounds, while the rest of the soldiers
fought for a few seconds, and then fell under
the great wave of furious Indians.

A strange change came to the youth when Curly saw the great chief, Conquering Bear, dying, his body bullet ridden, his head like a skull with the skin yellow and tight over it, and knew that the white men had done this thing because of the quarrel over the foolish cow. Curly felt the loss to his people like a loss to himself, and saw darkly the days of trouble ahead as more and more of the Wasichus came like seeds brought on the wind.

In the days that followed he had to travel with his band, as they left Fort Laramie and headed for wilder country to the north, and, in the rush, he and Bear Boy had time only for a hurried handshake in parting. The two hoped it would not be too long before they saw each other again, but it was to be a long time!

Daily he had sung his Dawn Song, and his Song to the Twilight, songs of the Roundness, prayers to the Spirit in the Silence, but now he lifted his voice with new urgency until he felt his soul lifting up to the Great One Above like the sun-flight of Wanbli Galeshka, the Spotted Eagle. Soon something called to him, something asking him to find an answer, to see in vision what he should do. So he rode his horse slowly into the heights until he found a pit left by an old eagle hunter long ago, and here he laid his body down on pebbles of stone and put some between his toes to keep away sleep that he might turn his mind sleepless to the blue sky of day and the star-sparkling sky of night and find a vision. He knew he was doing this without the usual preparation of the sweat bath and the ceremonies, but his mind was upset and seeking. He had to know the answer now.

Three days he stayed in the hills chanting the ancient chants to the seven directions, crying his desire for help to the One Above. He grew weaker from lack of food and water, fighting to hold his mind from wandering, but seeing no visions. He wondered about the white people, the Wasichus, who they were and why they came with their guns and beads and pale, sickly looking women and their lies. What could the Indians do about them? What should they do? What should he do? And he moved with voiceless anger when he thought of how some of his own people whispered that he himself had blood of the Wasichus in him! How could they say such things when they knew his father, a medicine man, and his mother, the sister of his real mother, a Brulé-Lakota who had died?

Twice the sun blazed in the blue sky and passed over to its sleeping place beyond the western hills, and the white stars wheeled twice across the dark blue of space, but still no dream came. At last he staggered to his feet late in the third day and walked weakly down from the hill, hunting for his hobbled horse and finding it finally in a little hollow where he collapsed against a cottonwood, the sacred talking tree, too exhausted to climb on his horse. And here he fell asleep, leaning against that tree.

There his dream came to him like lightning paling the darkness of distant clouds, sometimes in a fog of dimness, sometimes almost as

light as day, often filled with whirling shapes
and the song of bullets whining in war, and
always one who rode and thought and did
things with a mind that seemed to be part of
Curly. But he woke out of this dream with two
men shaking him and fought them wildly until
he saw they were his father, Crazy Horse, and
Hump, both very angry because they thought
a foolish boy had got himself lost in a place
where enemy Pawnees or Crows might soon find
him. When he tried to tell them he had gone
seeking a vision, they were still more angry
because he had not taken the purification of the
sweat lodge and the sacred pipe rites before
going. And then he was very angry himself
within, with a deep hurt that he hid behind a
face like rock, for did he not know in his heart
that he had seen a great vision? And about this
vision we will learn later when the time is right.
Hou! It is true what the wind brings to us from
the hills!

Now in darkness and in light a man may see
his future, but when he first sees it and until he
understands it and what he should do about it,
it hangs over him like a vast cloud and there is
fear in that cloud as well as a great calling. And
so it was with Curly from that day on until his
mind cleared and he knew his destiny. So he
became very quiet and withdrawn and went
often alone into wild places, until the people
called him "strange" and wondered why he did
not do the usual things of young men. But they
did not know the burden that lay upon him or
that he would live one day to be a great light in
their darkness!

Chapter 3

Out of the east comes danger

When a boy has dark thoughts and searchings he turns first to his mother if she is close to him. The one Curly called "Mother" was not his real mother, for she had died long ago when he was too little to remember. But this mother was her sister and also of the Brulés, a sister to the great Brulé Chief Spotted Tail. She must be like my mother, he thought, because she is more quiet than most women and she works hard to make the tipi comfortable, and the food good. He looked at her good, calm, strong face and the crinkles of laughter around the clear dark eyes and felt comforted. It was from her that he had learned the meaning of the good Lakota family life, for it was she who built the warm love and unity that surrounded the man, Crazy Horse, and his two sons and daughter, she whose touch was tender on a hurt, she who murmured in comforting agreement when her husband spoke of the great things of the

27

spirit but who disagreed with him sometimes
in a clear but kindly voice when he thought
young Curly should be punished severely for
what she considered only a small boy's mistake.

So there were no loud quarrels in that tipi,
no shrill whining of the nagger, no angry
throwing of pots and pans as he had seen where
the wife and warrior had not learned the good
Lakota spirit way. My father and mother, how
wonderful they are, he thought often, for they
talk things over and then decide, not one trying to outshout the other like a pair of prairie
dogs chittering over a grass blade.

She is a holy woman, my mother, he thought,
for in the long ago, in her girlhood, he knew she
could stand in the sacred way of girlhood and
was untouched by man. How different from
what happened in some of the Brulé and
Oglala and other Lakota camps now where the
white men, soldiers and others, had bought too
many maidens for a night of pleasure by pay-
ing a bolt of bright cloth, or strings of pretty
beads. How strange is the sickness that has
fallen on my people, he thought, for it was not
such for the many years after the White Buffalo Calf Maiden taught our girls the purity of
the spirit. Somehow the Wasichus have trapped
their minds and we must free them from these
traps once more.

He could not tell his mother about his vision,
for this was to be told only to a holy man, but
he could sit quietly by the fire and smell the
good smells of buffalo meat grilling or the sweet
wild scent of the onions and greens she had
picked for supper, and see her hands moving

quietly, efficiently to make these good things ready. And then one evening she spoke to him from a depth of womanly wisdom:

"My son, you are troubled by the white men and what they are doing to our people. I know you see what the Minne-wakan, the alcohol, is doing around the forts and trading posts, and how our young people are too often leaving the good Lakota way because of the lure of the white man's pretty things and his power. I know you have been seeking for help from the Great Spirit, and I am proud of your seeking. Let me urge you to continue seeking, but let me also ask you not to get too disturbed by what you find. Remember you are always of the far-vision people and not of those of little vision. There are few like you in this world, but you will live to see even beyond all the bad things and the bad times until the world comes back into the Circle of the Roundness and the Greatness comes again."

"But," the boy asked, "what about the terrible wagon guns of the white men that can destroy many men at a blow; and their faces that I hear swarm to the east of us as numerous as the leaves of the trees?"

"They may cover our country like the grasshoppers," she replied, "and bury our warriors beneath the waving grass and make our people weak and divided in the spirit as they are doing already, but this is only the passing of a long, dark shadow across the sun. The Great Spirit has made the circle of our people and He will make it again, if only a few, or even one, shall keep the dream alive like a hot coal carried from camp to camp for the fire. For one day He who knows all things will spring men and women of honor from the earth, and they shall be heroes spreading the fire into the hearts of all. You and I, my son, will never see that day, but I see that your name will be on their lips when they come and your spirit stand before them in the mountains, for you will have left a trail of light in this darkness and it shall be a guide to our people and perhaps to all people."

He looked at her in amazement, for she was staring into the fire and her eyes were full of little lights like one in a trance so that he knew, as sure as his hand touched his arrow, that she had just seen a vision, perhaps as great as his vision.

So the boy—for after all, he was still only a boy—left the fire of his mother with his heart cleared, though his mind still waited for more answers, and he went out into the camp with the other teenagers to race up into the hills on the backs of the wild ponies looking for antelope and buffalo, or to play the war games of pulling each other off the horses at full gallop. And he even walked through the deep grass to the canyons where the women and girls were picking summer cherries so that he could pick some himself and throw the pits at Black Buffalo Maiden, a pretty girl, the niece of Red Cloud. He had long ago brushed flies from her laughing round face as it bobbed in the cradle board on her mother's back as the camp moved. And since last summer he had watched her shyly, though she kept her face away from him until he managed to catch her on the cheek with a well-aimed pit, causing her to look up suddenly and meet his eyes. He knew with gladness that she was not angry. But she looked down suddenly again in fear at her boldness, and the crimson raced up her cheeks even as he turned away himself to run from the laughter and jibes of the older women.

But he kept it as a secret, deep in his heart, the way she had looked, and how she had moved among the bushes, lithe and graceful as a young doe with that wonderful light step of a girl of the Great Plains. There are girls and girls, he thought, but this is the girl for me. But his mother looked at him with pity when the tale came to her of that pit-throwing.

"She is a niece of Red Cloud," she said quietly, and prophetically, "and they have planned for her big things. They do not know your size in the spirit, nor will they know until it is too late."

He did not understand her words, or the darkness would have come to him again, but soon he was planning for a good visit with his cousins among the Brulés, and this too would be a turning point in his life.

After some months at one Brulé circle, he was riding one day toward another Brulé camp on the Creek of the Blue Waters, coming near after a long day's travel. The Thunders were talking in the west in the dark banks of clouds, and he listened to them always, for he loved the sound, even when they threatened that they might give him a soaking. But always the deep voices seemed to be calling, calling, like growling echoes of his dream, and the clean tang of the air they made and the hint of coming rain made him think of the Silent One. How beautiful the blue sky was in the east and how bright green the hills of spring, the circle of the earth and sky telling him of the circle the legends sang of, which would someday come for all men. And his heart filled with the bigness of all things, so that he hoped deep within that the smallness and the lies and the darkness that the white people seemed to be bringing were only a little thing after all, a winter storm that would die away as storms do into bright sunlight in the last days of the Moon of Shedding Hair.

Then his nose caught the smell of smoke and he dug his heels into the sides of the buckskin he was riding, for there was something about that smoke that told him it was not just made by campfires. So it was that he came through a light rain an hour later down to the Creek of the Blue Waters and saw the bodies lying there and the smashed tipis filled with bullet holes. And when he saw this his heart seemed to turn slowly over and over while a coldness descended upon him that he thought would never leave him. Men, women, and children lay everywhere, some of the little ones tossed and slashed on the sharp blades of the bayonettes. His anger gathered like the Thunders within him and he clenched his fists until the knuckles shone white against the brown skin. Now he began to see why his vision showed him riding through hails of bullets, and the dark war cries sounding around him like a thousand hawks shrieking in the sky.

Farther on he heard a soft cry and lifted up

part of a pile of buffalo robes to find a mother whom he recognized, Yellow Woman, a visitor from the Shyela (the Cheyennes), hiding with her baby beneath the pile. And he took them with him in sadness and anger back to his people, the Oglala, but remembering that he himself was half Brulé, and that it was the Brulé who had been attacked that day so ruthlessly. He also was part Cheyenne and felt keenly for these people who had visited in the circle of his Brulé relatives and met with disaster.

It was later that he learned how the attack had come in the early dawn, without warning, without meaning except the bitter white army's trick to smash the spirit of the people. And he heard how his uncle, Spotted Tail, had seized a sword from a soldier and cut down thirteen men in battle. But that one brave Brulé, whose deed symbolized those of many others, had not the force of mechanized and hardened professional killers, far away from home and family. He soon learned how Spotted Tail, still wounded from the fight, had given himself up to save his people whose homes were not far away, but close to every battle. Spotted Tail had been led away in chains with other chiefs to what many were certain was death. They were being taken as hostages to "white man's land." And now the white man wanted the land of all people. And where would it end? For a while, in the hot rushing of anger, Crazy Horse had forgotten the vision of his mother and forgotten the young white boy who was his blood brother.

Chapter 4

The meaning of a vision

From 1855 to 1858 was the time Young Curly was learning to be a man and warrior. His father and mother and Hump were watching him and sensing his moods and guiding him by a lifted hand here, a quiet word there, a bit of good food, and the warm strength of their presences.

It was a good time, for mostly the white people were far away and the Hunkpatila branch of the Oglala, old Crazy Horse's and Man Afraid's and Hump's band, had decided to leave behind forever the way of the Waglukhe, the loafers about the forts, Lakotas too close to the sweet food, the whisky, and the influence of the white soldiers at Fort Laramie and elsewhere. So they were out in the wild country most of the time where the air was clean, and the plains still likely to be dark with buffalo herds, or amber and white with the forms of antelope flashing over the prairie. How beautiful were the rolling swales in the Moon of Tender Grass and how lush for the ponies and the buffalo in the Moon of Shedding Ponies when the Hunk-patila band of the Oglala prepared for the first great buffalo hunt at the beginning of the Moon of Making Fat.

So the three older ones watched Curly quietly and they saw that he was turning into a youth who would become a man far different from the others.

He did not seem to like to dance or sing or dress himself up in fine skins and feathers and other decorations as the other young men would, especially when courting girls. Always he was quiet and often he liked to go off alone, especially to some lonely hill where the junipers reached out their gnarled forms against the winds of storms. Yet in the semi-war games of the young men, often played on horseback at full gallop and seeking to pull the "enemy" off his horse, he was astonishingly quick, wiry, and muscular so that, despite his boyish slender form, he was able to hold his own with much stronger youths. Always it seemed that a vibrant flame leaped within him, and his younger brother, Little Hawk, followed his every move with adoring eyes.

The old ones noted that he touched the leaves of the blue grass of the plains with fingers that delicately felt every rib; that he would lie still for hours watching the quail leading their young through the brush, or the courtship dance of the prairie chickens when the males flashed and pirouetted and strutted with their great fans of feathers as the females modestly

bowed their heads in admiration. They knew
he was absorbing the feel of the spirit that lies
behind every living thing even as a thirsty child
drinks in the cool crystal waters of a spring,
and they knew, as the far-seeing ones always
know, that one day he would be a holy man of
his people, one who would draw from all good
things of earth and sky the wisdom of the Center of Being.

Around the fire at night they discussed the
dreams of the family and the greater dreams
and songs of the people, the secret sacred
things that few white people ever learn about
because they have forgotten the way the Great
Spirit whispers in the night wind or the way
the world of dreams can lead us on the feet of
our breath into new wisdom if we but let it.
And because this knowledge can grow only in
an atmosphere of faith that is killed by the
crush of material things, the shock of too much
war, and the queer disease of the white men,
called "desire for money," it is very rare today.
Crazy Horse and his family, Hump and other
pure-hearted ones of the people who came to
visit, discussed how already the Waglukhe, the
loafers about the forts, had completely forgotten these things and were following the white
man's way like buffalo stampeding over a cliff
to death on the rocks below. So would all the
people if the darkness spread.

"We are learning," said Hump one day, "how
the prophecy of the great holy man, Drinks
Water, is coming true. He said strangers would
come out of the east and they would drive the
animals into the earth until most would disap-

pear, and drive our people into square gray houses where their spirit would die. So has it been happening already to some of our people, and so have the buffalo disappeared to the east of us and are getting less every year under the white men's guns. And at the Blue Water the white man showed us how he goes to war. He strikes to kill and destroy. He has no mercy for the weak ones and the little ones.

"Our wars between the tribes have been more like games. It is braver to touch a man than to kill him, and we have honored men of bravery even among our enemies by adopting them or letting them go free. If a few die we consider the loss with respect, and the wiser of our chiefs have helped us make peace so there was not too much killing. Our people have had plenty to share with brothers and sisters of other tribes until now. There is not land enough now, it seems, for even one tribe. We will have to learn a new way of war if we are to stop the white men from taking all our country."

Curly listened to the talk carefully, drinking it in and thinking about it when he lay on his couch of dried grass or sometimes the sweet-scented needles of the pines and the dying coals sent their glow against the poles of the tipi or the soft inner sides of the buffalo skins. Softly he sang his songs to Wakan Tanka, the Great Spirit, and wafted them in his mind up to the night sky where the stars wheeled across the darkness, telling the tales of heroes and animals. And he wondered about his dream of battles that someday he must tell to his father or one of the holy ones, and the dream of his mother that one day Wakan Tanka would make the hoop of the people whole again and even bring all the world into the circle.

But Black Buffalo Maiden, the niece of Red Cloud, also occupied his thoughts, especially when he saw her new, graceful ways as she brought water from the creek in the carriers made of buffalo stomachs, or laughing and playing the games of maidens. Once in a while he would catch the flash from her eye as she turned ever so slightly when he sped past her, horse and rider eager to join the hunt.

And at last came the time when he watched her with pride at a feast given by her family to honor her coming of age, and the nights when he stood in line with other young hunters and warriors, and took his turn to put his blanket around her, drawing her and himself into the sacred secret circle that might lead to wifehood and family. The words between them were few, but they were sweet in his heart and mind.

But his father and mother knew the danger in the hand of the niece of Red Cloud. Her parents dreamed of a marriage of power to one who would be rich and bring status, not to the strange son of a poor but honorable medicine man and hunter. So Curly was advised to visit and hunt with his cousins among the Shyelas and to see Yellow Woman again, she whose life he had saved at the Blue Waters. And they hoped secretly in their hearts that he would find a girl there, perhaps the slender younger sister of Yellow Woman.

"Yes, I will go to see the Shyelas," agreed

Curly. "Among them are relatives who still have fighting spirit." He had been told that his uncle Spotted Tail and the other Brulé leaders who had been taken to prisons in the east had been frightened by the size of the army and of ammunition supplies and by the numbers of white people in the cities. This great warrior uncle, who had swept thirteen blue-clad troopers from their horses with a sabre at the Blue Water, had come home from the distant white prison filled with talk about the vast armies of whites and the impossibility of fighting them.

So Curly went south with some Shyela friends who had been staying among the Oglala, until they reached the Solomon River in what is now northeast Kansas in the Moon of Colored Leaves. Here, in a fine Shyela camp, Yellow Woman hugged him as a mother would and her younger sister looked at him with sky friendliness. Ice, one of the great Cheyenne medicine men, talked to him like a father to a son, about the sacred things

He played games with the boys and teased the girls with a new sense of freedom, for the girls walked alone here, without women guarding them as among the Lakota; but each wore the sacred rope that was a sign of maidenhood and could not be broken without the man who broke it dying.

So did these people follow the sacred way of the Spirit, taught them long ago by Sweet Medicine, the Holy One, who was to the Cheyennes what the White Buffalo Calf Maiden was to the Teton Lakota.

Now came the time of the short white days

in the Moon of Popping Trees and through it
and the moons of Frost in the Lodge, the Dark
Red Calves, and the Moon of Snow Blindness,
Curly played the ice and snow games with the
girls and boys of the Cheyennes until he
became as expert as they were at the skating
and sliding, the running and leaping, the
throwing and dodging. And he liked the Cheyenne girls and waited to speak with some of
them on the trails to the lodges, but his heart
was still far away to the north with Black Buffalo Maiden.

By the Moon of Making Fat in 1857, the
Cheyennes were worried again about the white
men, and Ice and Dark, the two greatest of
their medicine men, prepared a medicine to
guard against bullets if their people were
attacked. After the first ceremonies, the drums
began to beat the solid roaring sound that
echoed in the hills and came back in answering
thunder. As the beat went on and Curly
watched the dancers swirling and leaping, moving in the proud way of old, the sound tuned
into his heartbeat and then the very beat of the
universe itself became part of that deep sound,
those swaying feathers and pounding brown
legs. The circle of dancers became part of the
circle of earth and sky, sacred with the meaning of spirit from the One Above.

But near the end of the Moon of Cherries
Reddening, Curly was to see those same strong
warriors he had seen dancing in the sacred way
melt before a charge of sabre-wielding white
cavalry as the snow melts in the first hot sun of
spring. Something went wrong. The warriors

went forth without bows or guns because of the ceremonies to stop the bullets, but the soldiers of Colonel Sumner used not the bullets but the shining steel of sabres that flashed in the sun and then turned red with blood as the mounted white men drove the Indians from the Solomon River and southward, fleeing in panic. The women abandoned their lodges and buffalo robes to the enemy, weeping when they saw the smoke rise from the fired village.

So again Curly had seen the white men destroy an Indian village with little resistance and he rode back to his people that summer, to the great Council of the Teton Lakota at Bear Butte, with his heart black with anger and sorrow and his mind wondering what his people could do. Still hope rose again when he saw the seven circles of the Teton Lakota, the Oglala, the Brulé, the Minneconjou, the Hunkpapa, the Two Kettles, the Blackfoot, and the Sans Arc, raising their tipis below the sacred mountain, Bear Butte, which rose like a great humped bear against the blue sky. Lakota horses covered the surrounding green waves of the summer plains like clouds of black dots, and the roar of the great drums filled the nights wih thunder.

Here he was proud to see all the famous warriors and chiefs gathered. Even his Uncle Spotted Tail of the Brulés stood tall among the others, while still warning of the white men coming like the locusts on the eastern winds. But there were still plenty of the war chiefs also, such as the seven-foot Touch the Clouds, with his famous father, Lone Horn of the

North, of the Minneconjous; the Oglalas' own
chief, Man Afraid of His Horses and the rising
Red Cloud; the withered Four Horns of the
Missouri country and his great nephew, Sitting
Bull of the Hunkpapas; Crow Feather of the
No Bows; and Long Mandan of the Two Kettles. And Curly was proud when he saw the
way they all turned to speak politely to his warrior father, Hump, tales of whose courage and
wisdom in battle had spread far.

When the chiefs walked down the line
between the gathered people, whose lives
weighed so heavily on their lives that no Itanca
(leader) would any longer know a single night's
peaceful sleep, their moccasins touched Mother
Earth together like one man, and their unity
symbolized the circle of all the Teton Lakota,
one nation in the Sacred Hoop. "Let the white
men come now," thought Curly. "If we keep the
circle, we can sweep them from the plains!" But
his mother touched his hand and he saw in her
eyes the warning of the far-seeing ones: "This
is not to be," the eyes said, yet the boy did not
want to believe her.

Then his eyes swept their gaze up to the top
of Bear Butte, that lonely outshoot of the Paha
Sapa, like a great bull buffalo leading a way for
the dark herd behind him to new pastures.
And prophetically, he thought, "Someday I shall
climb to that sacred place and find out the
future of my people!"

After the chiefs had pledged their strength
to holding the land of the Tetons, and after the
buffalo skin tipis had been taken down from
around the seven circles, and after the poles of

the great central lodge had been stripped and left bare to the winds that would howl out of the west in winter, Curly and his father went alone into the hills to the south of Bear Butte. It was the end of the Moon of Calves Growing Black Hair and the two found companionship in gathering the last of the fall fruits to add to their dried buffalo meat as they traveled. This was a journey together that the father had long planned, a journey to the place of his son's birth, and a part of his own seeing of the future of this strange youth who had come from his loins and the womb of that many-years-gone Brulé mother.

So they came to a high place the father selected, a place that looked down into a beautiful vale of Rapid Creek near the place where Curly had been born. The father took out his pipe from the long red-hair fringed carrying case, red-and-blue beaded, and filled with the sacred kinnikinnik and red willow bark, and smoked it to the seven sacred directions, once each to the west, the north, the east, and the south, once up to Father Sky, once down to Mother Earth, and once to the center of his being, for it is only by merging with all that the smallness of the man can become great.

After the ceremony the father continued to smoke silently, looking down by the creek where the willows flamed in gold, and a doe and her half-grown son came to sip from the shallows. He needed her less now, in fact she had difficulty keeping up with him. So quiet and peaceful it was that late afternoon, so mellow with the dying warmth of day that sky and earth seemed fused in unearthly beauty as if the Heart of the Silence were singing in the soft distant murmur of water and the still softer whisper of the wind through the needles of a lonely pine.

"My son," said Crazy Horse at last, "you have seen the gathering of the seven sacred circles of our people. It is the last time you and I will see this. There are bad times coming. Our thoughts must rise like the eagles or they will sink into the dust and be less than the burrowing of the gophers. The death of our people is already in our nostrils like the stink of the place where the vultures come. Our people need leaders capable of seeing beyond the sky to the One Above and getting His powers, for whatever is to come to us in darkness, there must still be light to guide us and guard us. A very great vision is needed and the man who has it must follow it even as the eagle seeks the deepest blue of the sky."

He was silent and Curly also was silent, fighting fears that rose within him like dark waves, for was he not only a small man among the warriors, so much smaller than the great chiefs like Touch the Clouds and Spotted Tail? But it was as if the voice of his father continued within him, whispering that a man's size meant nothing in the eyes of the Great Spirit, only the strength of his heart that beat with courage and the will that rose like fire and steel to drive the body wherever it was most needed. So he stood straight at last and dropped his blanket, sending out the power as Hump had taught him, so that he did not shiver in the cool fall air but lifted his spirit to the circle of All That Is and became one with it.

The father saw and understood, and without needing words to tell him, began to build the sacred sweat lodge down by the creek where water could be thrown on red-hot rocks to make the purifying steam. And in that steam later they talked not as father and son, but as a warrior would speak to a holy man, telling truthfully the tale of his vision and seeing even beyond the vision to the reality of all things that arc.

So Curly told of how he had seen a man on horseback, a horse that changed its colors through a swirling mist as if it were of many kinds, but which carried that man into dark storms of battle where the passage of bullets and arrows were like trails of fire always, fading, however, before they struck the man. And Curly felt and thought as that man felt, and knew that even as some of his people followed him into those storms of death, others reached out hands to try to hold him back. But there was a light that followed his movements, a light that pulsed and glowed, sometimes almost swallowed by the surrounding darkness, but then blazing up again even as the sun bursts from a cloud. And the man who was to become Crazy Horse had a little round dark sacred stone fastened under one ear, a single feather in his hair, a sparrow hawk flying over his head, his body streaked with lightning and the white marks of hailstones.

The father listened carefully and said at last when the story of the vision was finished: "This is indeed a great vision, and you must do as this man did, leading your people in spite of those who try to hold you back and the fading of the light. No bullet shall strike you from the enemy, for you have a sacred mission, and what this is, is beyond your eyes and mine but has some great meaning for our people and perhaps for all people, as your mother said.

"Never fear the darkness around you, no matter how great it may become, for it is doomed to pass away and be no more when the meaning of your life and that of all living things becomes clear. Somehow the coming of the white men is not the end of our people as it sometimes seems to us, but the beginning of something bigger than any of us can imagine. But go to the mountaintops, my son, to pray and fast whenever the spirit moves you, for there you are near to the Silent One and He will speak to you when you need help."

The two also were silent then for a long time and Curly knew that, though there was a great drought ahead, even as melting snow begins its trip to the sea so also from the mountaintops the water of his spirit would someday find its way to the Great Sea.

Chapter 5

Early war trails

In 1858 and 1859 the moons were busy times for Curly, in his midteens, now, and preparing himself to become a full warrior and going on his first war trails with Hump and other leaders of his people. Remembering his vision he went into battle without fear, but in his first big battle with a group of strange Indians on top of a high hill, he forgot the part of his dream that spoke against taking scalps. He killed two men bravely, but stooped to take their scalps and was shot in the leg by an iron-pointed arrow. He escaped by running down the hill, and when he reached Hump he threw the scalps away. Never again would he claim credit for killing by taking scalps.

At the village they sang of the bravery of the warriors, especially Curly, and his mother was glad to show the two scalps that Hump had saved. But Curly felt very sad over his forgetting to obey his vision until he heard his father walking through the village singing "The Song of a Good Name."

My son has fought a strange people;
he has been brave in battle.
Now I can give him a new name, the name
his father bore, and given to many
fathers before him.
I pass to him a great name.
He shall be called Crazy Horse.

Soon a great twin line of people, singing and laughing, came to the lodge of the new Crazy Horse. Far into the night they danced the dance of the new name and the new warrior born to the Oglalas, and the new Crazy Horse slept with a different sense of restfulness from having evidence now of what had so long been hidden. His father humbly took the name of Worm.

And not long later, Black Buffalo Maiden had her own ceremony as one become a woman and blessed by the Holy One for wifehood and motherhood. In the Moon of the Dark Red Calves, the old camp crier passed around the village announcing the big event for the pretty niece of Red Cloud. In beautiful white buckskin, with wing sleeves of blue, her black hair shining smooth and braided, her breast hung with bright beads of many colors, and her face painted vermillion, she sat on a pile of buffalo robes in the open front of her father's lodge. And all came to see her and hear the old village crier sing out the accomplishments and virtues—bead-working and diligence, good cooking and purity, skin-making and honor, and

above all, the good motherhood to her children
and to the people which she could have if she
would learn from Mother Earth of feeding, shel-
tering, and the silence that heals. Curly was
sure she brightened redder under her vermillion when she saw him watching her! And he
remembered when he had rocked her cradle
board when she was a baby until she smiled
and chortled in delight, and the times he had
watched her play as a laughing little girl, and
the time she had blushed when he threw the
cherry seeds at her in her first budding of
womanhood. Yet there were other young men
looking at her longingly now, and one was No
Water, a young warrior of a family with many
horses and honored relatives, upon whom the
mother of Black Buffalo Maiden looked with
smiling eyes.

As the moons passed, the people saw that
although the new Crazy Horse was indeed a
great warrior, first in the ranks of the warriors
in the fights against the Crows, the horses he
brought back were usually given to the poor
people, especially those who came back disillu-
sioned from the loafers' camps at the edges of
the white man's forts, and that he kept only two
or three for war. No Water, the brother of Black
Twin, and a relative of Old Smoke, had many
more horses, and his costumes were always rich
with beads, his gun new and of the latest kind.
They said he alone of the young men was
allowed past the guarding mother at any time
to enter the tipi and talk to Black Buffalo
Maiden. But Crazy Horse heard also that the
girl would not speak to No Water, and he was

comforted, sure that she was waiting for him. Yet to claim her he would need to bring many horses for one who was the niece of Red Cloud.

For three, four, five winters now and summers too, most of the Oglala had been away from the forts, under the good leadership of Man Afraid of His Horses, and others like Hump and Red Cloud, leading the old plains Indian life, free of the whisky and the frustrating waiting on more white man's lies and rations. It was good to rise in the morning in a free village of the open country full of sacred places known to the generations, and to run down to the nearest stream for a dip and prayer just as the sun rose.

It was good to hear the laughter of the people and see the women busy with the new skins of buffalo, deer, and antelope or an occasional elk, to see the hunters come in heavy-laden, and the girls bringing baskets full of bright berries in the Moon of Cherries Black. It was good to see the unity of the people under the Sacred Tree, that Spirit Tree woven out of the sacred ceremonies and the sacred pipe. This was the Sacred Tree to which Sun Dancers were linked by rawhide vowing to live and breathe with that tree for the people. So here there were no lies, no broken promises, no drunken brawls, no stealing for money or whisky, no girl favors bought for a night, with new blankets or beads. There was only the clear of the blue sky, the sparkling streams, the clean camps, the rhythm of the great drums, the black herds of the buffalo and the dawn songs rising with the first rim of the sun. It was good to be alive.

But the news from distant places was not good. For a hundred miles on either side of the holy road, where the Wasichus drove their cattle and wagons across the dusty plains of the Platte, almost all game was now gone. To the east everywhere the buffalo were disappearing, until only their bones lay whitening upon the plains, so that the old men talked of what should be done to save them in the Teton Lakota country. And all knew the Wasichus were coming closer, closer, like a dark sickness rising out of the east. What could be done?

Young Crazy Horse, with thoughts of a good life promised by the seedling love he felt could grow between him and Black Buffalo Maiden, thoughts that were with him even when he was gone on the war parties against the Crows and the Shoshones, felt this dark cloud in the back of his mind, but tried to shove it away. Subconsciously he did this, as a man does swimming long in a sea and feeling the tide pulling at him and hoping it will calm. So do the young think for a while more strongly of the bright sun and leaves and a pretty face and forget for a little the great and demanding dreams.

His father and mother watched him and knew what was in his mind, but were patient.

The young man breathed into the nostrils of the horses he captured, the bays, the golden ones, and the others, breathing his spirit into them in the way of old, and rode them until he felt their spirits merging with his on the long trails and the hunts, the war-charges and the flights from too many bullets. So, in the Moon of Making Fat in 1861, when the white men far to the east were getting ready for the first battle of the Civil War at Bull Run, young Crazy Horse was on a war party against the Snakes or Shoshones, under Washakie, their greatest chief, at a camp on the Sweetwater. The Lakota charged past the camp to the herd of horses beyond and cut out four hundred of the best, whooping them over the ridge toward Lakota country. Then Crazy Horse and seven others stayed behind to fight off the pursuit, seeing a brave thing, the charge of the young son of Washakie, with two hand guns blazing, cutting down two Oglala, but going down himself under the spears of the others. And they knew later that he had done this rash thing because of the angry words of his father, accusing him of cowardice when he had been a little slow about joining the fight. So was the heart of the old man broken and so do the old wish too late that they had been kinder to the young, for fibres of greatness are not strengthened by ridicule.

Soon, over the intervening ridges and by a small wood where the Lakota gathered to stand off the pursuit of the angry father, young Crazy Horse was doing a foolish thing himself, charging on foot across the plain to put out of its misery a horse screaming its death cries in a buffalo wallow and trying to stagger to its feet. Always did he hate to see the weak and helpless in pain, and came when he could to help them. But the old warriors shook their heads over his wild run across that plain, and the fall of the war club that crushed the dying horse's skull to end that keening cry. Again the bullets and arrows were flying around him, but their passage was only shadows that never touched him.

He could feel their movement against him, like something coming, but moved his body lightly from side to side like a boy dodging tossed cherry pits in children's games.

Warriors were rushing to count coup on his running form, but a Shoshone on horseback who was charging the woods did not see him and young Crazy Horse's club swung again, this time to claim a man, and he sprang into that empty but sweat-slippery saddle and was off to his friends before the Snakes could catch him. "Strong medicine!" the old ones exclaimed. "But he should use it for something better than killing a wounded horse!"

So young Crazy Horse came back to the Oglala camp with a new repeating rifle and a beautiful sorrel war horse, but he did not join in the victory dance, nor did he even try to visit Black Buffalo Maiden. He is too shy, his father thought, but his mother shook her head, whispering to herself: "The girl is not for him. The powers have willed it so," but not saying it, for she knew Worm wished his son to find a wife now that he was a renowned warrior.

That winter (early 1862) the trader's sons came in the Moon of the Dark Red Calves and the Moon of the Snow Blindness to trade with the people blankets and axes and guns, silver dollars and beads and needles, for the beaver and fox furs, buffalo robes, and fine tanned deer skins. They were half-breeds, most of them, their mothers of the Lakota, and some had gone to the white man's school to learn to read. These brought papers printed in the east that told of the great war between the white people of the south and the white people of the north, and of the thousands and thousands of men killed in battle. And these they read to the people. Young Crazy Horse listened and hoped the white people would stay busy with their war and leave the Indians alone, but Worm and Hump said it was really bad because the whites were learning even more about how to kill and one day they would use this knowledge on the Lakota.

He did find time in the Moon of Tender Grass and the Moon of Shedding Ponies to travel to the camp of the Bad Faces (Red Cloud's band of the Oglala) to pay attention again to Black Buffalo Maiden and sometimes hold her inside the circle of his blanket. But others pushed and shoved for their cause, and he did not like to see No Water staying in the circle longer than he did, favored by the girl's father and mother. Once the girl's mother even tore the blanket away when she thought young Crazy Horse took too long, and that was a thing most shameful for the young warrior, the girl anxious after that for the blanket not to be about them too long. His mother shook her head when she heard the story.

"My son," she said, "the Bad Faces have chosen another man for this girl. You will be hurt if you keep after her." But young Crazy Horse was silent and his eyes looked longingly to the west.

Soon a great war party against the Crows

was planned, Red Cloud leading, choosing Black Twin and No Water from the Bad Faces. Hump was sent a message to come and bring the two sons of Worm, Crazy Horse and the younger Little Hawk, reckless and wild as usual, his long braids wrapped in bright weasel skin and his face red-painted. The older of the two, plain of face, a single feather in his hair, rode his fine red sorrel, won from the Shoshones and now prancing with pride, while Little Hawk climbed on a racing bay, so anxious to go he tore off across the plains ahead of all to show his fine horsemanship.

"*Hola!*" laughed Crazy Horse, "my brother dances the scalp dance before he has come close to the scalps!" Then more seriously, "But save your horse, Little Hawk, for the day when running really counts."

Shaking his lance and rearing his bay high on its hind legs, Little Hawk shouted back: "This horse and I will run down any Crow in the west. Catch up with me, brother, if you can, or there will be none of them left!"

Even the Bad Faces were glad when the Hunkpatilas arrived with so many good warriors, including also Young Man Afraid, son of Man Afraid, and Lone Bear, the women trilling the victory call as the whole party moved out of the Bad Face Camp, heading west to the land of the Crows. Many men were glad young Crazy Horse was along, for he brought good luck, and they knew he would leave no wounded man behind, but would dare to rescue any that were hurt.

They had hardly started out, however, before

No Water complained of a bad toothache, push-
ing his fist against his cheek and wincing at the
pain. They knew No Water's medicine came
from the two teeth of a grizzly bear, and that if
his own tooth was bad this warned of failure
for him coming. So No Water stayed behind
while the party went bravely against the Crows.

A week later they struck at dawn a large
hunting village of the Crows on the Powder
River, and the river mist was filled with racing
forms, then the wild cries of the attackers
plunging through the tipis, shooting at the rising warriors, and on to capture the horse herd.
The Crow warriors coiled and gathered like a
wounded rattlesnake, then struck back fiercely
to hold off the Lakota while their women and
older men got their tipis down and took off to
the east. In the running battle of all that day,
the Crows were driven eastward still fighting,
but their hearts lowered when an old man chief
fell, pierced by arrows. Beyond the Tongue and
even the Little Bighorn they were driven, but
they still fought and protected their weak ones.
So that at last Red Cloud shouted, "They have
been men! Let them go!" and the Lakota turned
back to their own homes. And all remembered
how young Crazy Horse and Little Hawk had
raced, in the heat of battle, after a wounded
Oglala deep among the Crow fighting men,
seizing him under the arms when they jumped
from their horses, and getting him carefully
and tenderly onto the back of the war sorrel,
where he could grasp Crazy Horse about the
middle and be carried to safety through a hail
of bullets and arrows.

Back at the camp of the Bad Faces, Crazy Horse was met by Woman's Dress, a man who had long been jealous of him, and who had been called as a boy "The Pretty One." Woman's Dress's dark eyes gleamed triumphantly as he reported, "My cousin, No Water, is walking under the blanket with one whom you know." Young Crazy Horse knew this meant that Black Buffalo Maiden was now Black Buffalo Woman and married. He stopped his horse and stood perfectly still as if struck by sky fire, his face turning pale as the moonbeams. If his hand had not been nerveless with shock, he would have drawn his knife and driven it swift as an arrow into the heart of Woman's Dress. But when he recovered, the man was gone, a malicious shadow, and the young warrior drooped like a winter-struck sunflower as he turned his horse sadly for home without a word or glance for his companions of battle.

Worm and his mother saw him coming from afar at the Hunkpatila Camp and the two knew instantly what had happened. No word was said as they opened the flap for him into the tipi, but they saw him fling himself down on his bed and lie as if dead. Gently the father closed the door and walked silently and sadly away with his wife to the tipi of High Horse, his brother. There they would stay until the young man was ready to face the world again, but the mother could not help muttering, "I told him the girl loved power and wealth better than the love of a good warrior!"

So also the voices ran through the camp like the little breezes among the women. They talked of how Red Cloud had had his way again, and maybe the whole war party was a trick to get Crazy Horse away while the girl was married to one who would help the leader of the Bad Faces with the power he needed.

In three days' time, young Crazy Horse noticed that his father had covered brush over the door of the tipi to guard his son from prying eyes and disturbance, and he wept a little in gratitude, the tears dropping down his hard brown cheeks. Then he shook himself like a great bear after battle, put powder and bullets into a sack for war, got on his red sorrel, lifted the noble head high, and pointed the flaming nostrils toward the east and north on the way once more against the Crows.

After that trip he became part of the camp again, a little more kind if possible than before to find a widow or an old man in need of meat or a horse, a little more silent as he listened around the campfire to the stories and legends. Some of the mothers with marriageable girls hoped he would be visiting their lodges, but he kept to himself and they could see he was thinking long thoughts, though not about their daughters.

For months No Water and Black Buffalo Woman stayed far away from the Hunkpatila camp, but one evening in the Moon of Colored Leaves, when the cirrus clouds were feathering their arrows across the western sky, Crazy Horse came riding by the camp of the Bad Faces and suddenly saw the young wife of No Water rising from behind a nearby clump of the fragrant sage bushes where she had been gathering potherbs. At first she threw her blanket over her startled face, but, when no harsh words sounded, she dropped it slowly and spoke softly:

"My father and my mother and my brothers said I had a duty—and you remember what the old wise one said about the duty of the daughter . . ." Her voice trailed away into the stillness and her face was suddenly helpless and quivering.

The young man raised his hand. *"Hou, Kola!"* he replied. "Let there be no bad words between us. I am no longer angry. You have chosen!" And he rode away into a growing silence, until the young woman took her basket suddenly and threw it with all its herbs as far as she could, then turned her head and wept.

Chapter 6

Storm clouds from the east

Eighteen-sixty-three to 1864 were years of uneasiness for the Plains tribes. The whites were still engaged in a tremendous war in the east, but in spite of this war, they were still moving into the west in increasing numbers. Crazy Horse and other leaders sensed that when the white war was over, the Indians' turn would come.

Strangely enough, some very fine young white men came to visit the Lakota at this time when agents, treaty commissioners, and cavalry seemed bent on giving the worst possible impression of white men. Among those who showed that there was honor even among white people were Casper Collins, the son of a soldier chief, and Thomas Carter, a former trader's son. Collins sincerely wanted to learn the Lakota language and the Indian way of life. Carter already knew much about the Indians, and could speak Lakota fluently. Crazy Horse met him one beautiful day in the Moon of Shedding Ponies. He saw a young man riding a pony over the distant plains with the flowing grace of an Indian, and was surprised when he came near to see the light hair, though his face was dark from the sun.

Holding up his hand, the stranger cried "*Hou, Kola!*" and his blue eyes sparkled with smiles. And suddenly Crazy Horse came together with him, pounding his back and hugging in the way only of great friends.

"*Matohoshila!*" he said, over and over. "Where have you been?" Bear Boy explained that he had been sent back east to schools, but he had always remembered he was a Lakota even though he had a white skin.

"And now," he said, "I have come for the Hanblecheyapi. It is time I become a man. Can you help me?"

Young Crazy Horse took him to see Worm and his mother, and then to see Hump, but Little Big Man, one of the young warriors, took a dislike to Bear Boy, saying: "No white man can take the Hanblecheyapi—it is for the Lakotas only!"

Crazy Horse did not have to speak. Hump fastened Little Big Man with the piercing glance of his eyes, saying contemptuously, "We call our friends by the color of their hearts, not the color of their skins. There are too many now among the Lakota who are following the white man's way of quarreling and drinking rather than the way of the Hanblecheyapi. But this young man is leaving the white man's way to become like us, a part of the circle. In the circle, all are brothers, regardless of the color of their skins."

And Little Big Man, short but chunky and strong as his name meant, sulked off by himself, his eyes growing dark as they followed the movements of Bear Boy.

Hump turned to Bear Boy, and spoke wisely: "Watch out for that one! He may put an arrow in your back. But remember I have accepted you now for what you did before. You must prove to my people that my trust in you is not wrong."

Bear Boy was silent, but he stood straight and proud, with his hands turned outward and his face to the sun. There was no need for him to talk, for they knew what he meant. So they took him into their lodges and laughed with him and gave him of the meat of the chase, roasted over the coals until the fine smell of buffalo tongues and elk steaks rose in the warm air of spring. The young white man was one with them, as in the past when young Curly had found him among the sand hills near Fort Laramie and painted his face and hair brown to make him look Lakota.

Soon it was the Moon of Making Fat, and young Casper Collins joined Bear Boy, Crazy Horse, and the Hunkpatila on a buffalo hunt. The hunters moved out in the good way of old over the plains near the Powder River, with the Akicita holding back the eager young men so the scouts, such as Crazy Horse and Hump, could give the signal for when the charge could be made. They saw in time, the herd, like black clumps on the rolling hills, near the river and gave the signal for the surround. At this, the hunters got off and led their horses slowly up to the ridge crests, then waved the blanket again for the charge, when every man was in his proper place.

Up and over the hills the Lakota hunters raced on their horses, a wild keening coming from their lips when the herd was struck. Some shot with bows and arrows and some with the new and old guns, and a few used the long lance of the ancient days, the lance that has to be held just right and driven between the ribs in the back of the shoulder at the right spot only or the bull or cow is likely to turn savagely and rip the rider from his horse.

The herd plunged away, the horses with men on their backs running among them, the dust clouds darkening the sun, and the smell of blood and sweat in the air. Bellowing filled the sky also and the wild shouting, the day great for a hunt, and the Akicita making sure any wounded buffalo was killed and not allowed to wander in pain; for the Indian knows the buffalo is his brother, even though he must kill him for food, clothing, and shelter.

Casper Collins and Bear Boy each had a bull down, with a bullet apiece, the red gore darkening the grass and the knives out for the skinning. Like the Lakota, they knew that each bit of animal that could be used must be saved, meat and even the intestines for the meals of the future, some eaten right away and some smoked and dried into jerky for the coming winter. The stomach made a fine waterproof bag for carrying water; the sinews from the backbone made thread for the women and bow-strings and bow-backing for the hunters; the bones could be made into tools and awls when the white man's steel was not available; the horns were used in the dances or for tools; the hoofs made a glue; the skins made tents, blankets, and robes; and even the tail could be used for a fly switch or sweeping out a tipi.

As Bear Boy bent over to start cutting away the skin, he heard a swish like a little sudden wind, and looked up to see an arrow sticking in the ground beside him. It had flown by where his upper body had been only a second before. When Crazy Horse came running up, Bear Boy pointed to the arrow, then to his body and lifted up to show where the arrow might have gone. Crazy Horse's eyes narrowed.

"Let us hope," he said, "that this was only an accident. But be on guard, my friend."

After the last meat of the hunt had been dried, the people had a time for leisure, and it was then that Worm prepared the Inipi and Hanblecheyapi ceremonies for Bear Boy. Worm explained them: "In the long ago seven ceremonies for the seven sacred circles were given to us, some by White Buffalo Calf Maiden, and some by Holy Ones long before her. By these ceremonies our people have life. Forgetting them, as is done by the Loafers about the Forts, means death for our sacred tree and sacred hoop and for our people. Each ceremony has special songs that go with it. All these ceremonies and songs come from the Great One Above. Your people also probably have sacred songs and ceremonies, but either they have forgotten how to use them, or they have lost their power because of the way the religion of the Wasichus is divided into little parts, each going a different way. Long ago our old ones told us that they knew a strange people would come out of the east and they might destroy our songs for a while, but that one day they would come back and instead of seven circles there would be nine. What this means I do not know. All I can do now is to teach you the meaning of these things so you will see why they are important to us and to the Great Spirit.

"Listen carefully. These two ceremonies, the Inipi and the Hanblecheyapi, are probably the most important of the seven; in fact we use parts of all the seven in these two so that when we only have time for two they contain the meaning and feeling of all. The Inipi ceremony is the purification ceremony to make you ready so you can go up on the mountain for the Hanblecheyapi. Sometimes when we talk to our young men and women about purification, they listen only with one ear, or none at all. This did not use to be, but has been happening since the coming of the Wasichus. This is because they are thinking about all the strange and wonderful things the Wasichus bring. They are dazzled as a fish is sometimes by the sunlight shining on the water, so that it is easy to catch it in the net. They forget that to the Great Spirit, guns and beads and pretty blankets mean nothing if the heart is not good. Even the talking wires, the telegraph, are only as good as the message that goes over them. If the messages on those wires do not lead to peace and goodness between people, but to lies and quarrels and wars, then it would be better if those wires had never been!

"In the Inipi ceremony you are to listen and watch and feel. Speak only when you are asked to speak, but be alert at all times. In the darkness of the sweat lodge, you may see the little blue lights if your heart is good and you are listening, but if your heart is bad and you do not believe, then those lights will be yellow. If they are yellow, it will be useless for you to have the Hanblecheyapi, for your heart will not be pure. Something bad will happen to you.

"What does it mean to be purified and pure? This is required of all of us by the Great Spirit if we are to help our people and our children's children. There is a darkness coming now because of many sick hearts or hearts that think only of themselves. But the Great Spirit will not allow this to last. Someday he will show all people how to become pure again. We must keep the light of purity alive even in this darkness. To be pure means to think only of good things and to do only good deeds. We cannot hurt other people if we are pure unless, of course, they are so sick they are a danger to all. We cannot tell lies. We cannot take things that do not belong to us. We cannot speak badly about other people, but help them by praise instead. We cannot think about girls and women with lust, but only with true love that surrounds them and protects them because they are the sacred givers of life, the mothers of the new children to be; and those children must be surrounded by love and strength, not lust and weakness, if they are to grow up to be good people. We cannot let either fear or hate enter into our hearts, for fear makes the blood turn to water and a strong man weak, while hate makes the blood too thick and causes the fool to strike without thinking. And above all we must be humble like the earth beneath our feet, for Mother Earth gives us all the green growing things and keeps the animals and us alive, yet she lets us walk upon her. So we do not hold ourselves too high with pride, but are kind and friendly to all people, looking for the good in them and helping it grow.

"When you are taking part in these ceremonies, pray always that your heart and mind will be pure and humble, that you will see the Great Spirit in all living things and will seek the power only to help others. Not for one second must you think of selfish or unworthy things, or even of your own desires, for you are building the great and good power to think always in the way the Lord of the Silence wishes you to think and to do only the things He wishes you to do. It is true you may later fail and falter, for you are human, but if you can maintain this purity during these ceremonies, then you can always look back on this time and say, 'Then I was good; I can do this again; help me Great Spirit!' and the Spirit will come to you if you are truly sincere.

"Remember also that all things used in these ceremonies are sacred, not for themselves alone, but because they symbolize the powers of the Great Spirit, even indeed as do the sky and the earth, the clouds and the mountains and the lakes. For example, the willows we use in making the sweat lodge still have their leaves on and symbolize the Great Spirit's power to make things grow, to die but also to be reborn again each spring. So is man's spirit a growing thing, dying eventually but also being reborn. The rocks we use are sacred to the everlasting nature of the Great Spirit; the water we put on them when they are hot to make steam is the water of life and spirit that cleanses our souls; the fire itself is the central symbol of purity, for in fire all may be purified of sickness and darkness of spirit. Look on all these sacred things as teaching you a lesson, and if you learn this lesson you will grow strong and good and become a great human being with great visions, but if you learn nothing you will become little and your spirit will pass away like a puff of smoke from a dying fire, without meaning or usefulness.

"When you go up on the mountain to cry for a vision, the Hanblecheyapi, you must go completely purified by the Inipi ceremony, so that the whole time you are on that mountain, having no food and maybe no water if the days are not too hot and dry, you will be sending out your spirit into the sky and down to the earth and out to the four directions like a great river flowing down from the hills, never stopping. And so your spirit will come into contact with the Great Spirit and He will speak to you through the birds or animals, or the clouds or the thunder, or the wind in the leaves of the trees, until you see or hear something that opens the way for you into the heart of the universe and you will become one with all things that live.

"Remember that there is a falling away from this searching among our young people. Even though the Wasichus are our enemies in many ways, the young men and women are drawn to their ways and the things they make, like flies to the dead body of a buffalo on the plains, and they are forgetting the old songs and the greatness of their people. I am hoping that you who are of the Wasichus, but who also want to be one with us, will be of help someday in turning our people back to the search for the Great Spirit that they need so badly, and your people also."

Crazy Horse and Worm were proud to see that Bear Boy listened with all his heart and that when he prepared for the Inipi ceremony he did all that he was told to do without a murmur. Worm was first in the sweat lodge to make the opening prayer, while young Crazy Horse, learning the way of the holy men, made the sacred fire at the end of the trench that faced the east. Here the hot rocks were prepared and later brought into the lodge after all had filed within, so that the water of life could be thrown upon them, along with the sacred sweet grass and sage to bring forth the fragrant steam. Four times the sweat lodge was made dark and four times it was opened up to light, to signify the four ages of the earth and the battle between light and darkness. Four times the water and the sage and sweet grass were thrown on the red-hot rocks to purify the bodies of those within the lodge and cleanse their minds also of all but spiritual things. And when the last darkness came so also came the little blue lights that moved about like disembodied ghosts from place to place, sometimes pausing for a moment before a dark dreaming face as if to see what was behind the eyes; but of yellow lights there were none, and Worm said the spirits found the lodge purified.

Carrying a buffalo robe and naked except for a loin cloth, Bear Boy left the Inipi ceremony for a nearby butte, riding a horse led by young Crazy Horse and followed by Worm. At the base of the butte they made the ceremony to the seven directions, smoking the sacred pipe, and Worm called on the powers of the Universe to help the young man who came crying for a vision. Thus was the Hanblecheyapi for Bear Boy begun, and he walked to the top of the butte where a place was prepared for him with a bed made of sagebrush, and a circle of the sacred tobacco, plus a small offering of dried meat and wild fruits to the Powers. Also five poles were put up, including a center pole and four poles for the four winds, each with a cloth, one red, one black, one white, and one yellow. Here he was told to circle to the directions, holding his pipe with the stem outward, pointing first to the west, then the north, east, and south, twice up to Father Sky, and once down to Mother Earth, making seven prayers or songs as he did so. And the main prayer he sang was:

"*Wakan Tanka onshimala ye oyate wani*

wachin cha!" (O Great Spirit, be merciful to me that my people may live!)

"Be of strong heart," said Worm as he left him, "and may your heart reach the Great Spirit because it is pure and good. Pray that you may have a vision of how to help your people and mine. When you have had a vision and wish to come down, lower the central pole and we will come for you. Otherwise we will come for you at the end of the fourth day."

The days passed and the pole was not lowered, but on the third evening a great dark cloud came out of the west full of the yellow streaks of lightning and loud with the roar of the Thunder Beings.

"This is a test," said Worm, "whether he will be strong. We will know when we see him whether his power was great, because there will be no sign of rain where he stands, though we can see now that it is pouring up there on the mountain."

On the fourth day they saw that all the poles were down, so they climbed up the rocks and came to where Bear Boy had been, but there was no sign of him, though all around the sacred place where he had been praying there was much sign of rain, but none where he had stood. They followed his tracks down the mountainside and found him sprawled on a large rock with a gash on his head where he had fallen in the darkness and been knocked unconscious. When his face was washed with water, the wound dressed, and a damp skin pressed to his lips, he came out of his deep sleep, muttering for a while as if he had lost his mind, but gradually his eyes cleared and he began to look at them intelligently, though his eyes were dark with something they could not understand.

They put him on a horse and brought him down to the camp, where the mother of young Crazy Horse put a soothing compact of wet medicinal leaves on his head, and, at last, he spoke.

"When the thunder and lightning came, I was afraid at first," he said, "but then I remembered that the spirit that is strong needs to fear nothing, and I prayed harder. Then I saw the hail falling near me, but none of it struck me, and I felt very strong, for I knew the Spirit was protecting me. I lay down while the Thunders were talking above me, and suddenly I was asleep. In my dream I saw a man lying on a rock with an arrow in his back, but not where the heart is, and I saw that he was alive and that he was me, but I knew he was dying and I felt very sad.

"Then, in another place, as if my eyes could see close up of something faraway, I saw another man lying with a wound in his back just as my wound had been, but without an arrow in it. He was an Indian, and he also was dying, but I could not see who he was. But around him I heard a great wailing.

"The wailing did not die for a long time. When it did, I was back with the man who was me lying near death. Below him was a canyon where a great river of people were walking, white people, with their faces turned toward the west, but they seemed not to be human beings, but all with their eyes fixed on something in the distance that held them like a magnet. Yet, now and then, one or two or three would pull their glances away from this thing and leave the great stream and start to try to climb out of the canyon to where the man who was me was lying.

"Then I heard the Thunders talking above me, but at first I could understand nothing of what they said, until gradually one voice seemed to be speaking to me and gradually I began to understand the words.

" 'They die on the trail of gold,' the voice said. 'They live and die for that which is nothing and the land shall become ugly because of what they do. They shall bring darkness on darkness, but after them shall come the light. Watch!'

"I watched and gradually those whose eyes were fixed on the west began to get smaller and smaller and around them a darkness was growing, but those who had left the march and were climbing the cliffs seemed to grow in size and around them came a light like a sunrise, gradually growing stronger. Then I saw the Lakota and other Indians above the white people who were climbing the cliffs, and they put down their hands and ropes to help those climbing so that even when they got tired they could make it all the way to the top. And the great voice in the Thunder spoke.

" 'It is good, the deaths shall not be in vain!'

"And that is all I knew until you woke me up and I found this wound in my head."

Young Crazy Horse and his father were silent for a very long time, and Bear Boy looked from one to the other in a strange way until at last Worm spoke.

"The Thunders gave you a sight into the future. You are to die, probably in battle, but you are also to live in the minds of men who will hear of your dream and listen. These are those who climb the cliffs of the spirit away from the white man's way that is destroying the earth, as we were told it would, long ago, by our great holy man, Drinks Water. You have sought the good Lakota spirit way of going to the mountain to pray and fast, and one day others like you of your people will seek that way too, but it is too early yet for that beginning. You and the Indian you saw in your vision, who also was wounded and dying, will die in the dark time, when many are forgetting the spirit, but both of you will help your people into a new day of light and harmony. Would that we all might live to see that day when your people and my people will come back to greatness! And it is good to know that in that time my people will help yours."

It seemed in the next month bad news followed on bad news. First came the Santee Sioux, drifting out of Minnesota with their tale of the bloody fight against the whites in 1862, when no food had been given to the Indians and they rose in frenzy. Some boasted of the white man's goods they had looted and the white prisoners they had bought, but it was obvious their boasts were empty because they had had to leave their home. Then the peaceful Yankton Sioux were attacked because of what the Santee had done, and Crazy Horse knew more women and children must have suffered. Still worse came news of what was happening in the south and north to their brother the buffalo. White hide hunters were swarming everywhere with repeating rifles, killing the buffalo in hundreds, ripping off the skins, but leaving the fine meat to rot in the sun or await the vultures and wolves. At this news Crazy Horse rose like a wounded grizzly and paced the floor of his father's lodge. "They are driving the buffalo and the other animals into the ground," he growled. "When the buffalo are gone how can our people live?"

He heard how the soldiers were swarming now on the Holy Road and how a new breed of soldiers had come, men who were close to the Gray Men, the thieves and cutthroats of the West, in their idea that Indians were little more than lice to be ground beneath their boots. He saw Little Hawk happily sharpening his hunting knife and war hatchet, and singing a song about blood soon to be let, but Crazy Horse remembered the day at the Blue Water when he had seen the cut-up bodies of women and children, and he could not be happy at the prospect of war, though he felt it coming like a great dark cloud.

Then worst of all in the ice-cold Moon of Popping Trees, 1864, came the news of the massacre of Black Kettle's Cheyennes, over four hundred of them and mostly women and children, at Sand Creek on the Big Bend of the Arkansas River, by Colonel Chivington of the Colorado Volunteers. The fact that these "soldiers," so called, had ruthlessly killed every Indian they encountered down to babies, and had cut off intimate parts of their bodies besides, drove the remaining free tribes of the plains wild with rage. That these peaceful Cheyennes, under a peace chief, Black Kettle, could be so easily killed when they were supposed to be under the protection of the white government sent the pipe of war from tribe to tribe like a great wind. What the Indians did not hear was that though Chivington and his men were first received in Western towns as conquering heroes, soon the tide turned as the real nature of their massacre of helpless children and women became clear, and more and more white people raised their voices against this outrage.

By that time it was too late, and Crazy Horse knew, as did other Indian leaders, that their peoples demanded revenge. The storm had come, the war was on!

The news came too late in another way also. Two days before the news of the massacre came to the camp of the Hunkpatila, Bear Boy had left the Oglalas to rejoin his parents at Fort Laramie. Now Crazy Horse left the camp to follow his trail, fearful that the young white man would be attacked before he knew what had happened far to the south. Though Crazy Horse raced his best horse to catch up with Bear Boy it was not until three days passed that he found him. Ah, indeed, it was too late, as the vision had spoken truly. Far off he saw the figure lying on the rock, and when he got close, there was the arrow in the back. A cry of rage rose in his throat, but there was no one near to vent his anger on, only the weak winter sun in the sky, and the blood congealing into ice on the rock. The young white man was not yet dead, but the birds of death were hovering close.

Crazy Horse knew it was useless and too painful to pull out the arrow. He took off his buffalo robe from his horse and spread it around the still figure, putting a bunched piece of cloth under his head for a pillow, and put his head low. The voice came so weakly that he could hardly hear it.

"My vision came true!" There was a hint of triumph through the pain, and even a little laughter. How could a man die so bravely, and such a good man! "It is Crazy Horse who has come, I know, my friend! My friend! If my death would only help you and your people, but I know that a longer darkness must come first before the light. Remember me when you too die, and do not curse my people. Remember that I love you, and one day there will be many of my skin who will love you too. For at last they shall understand that we are all men of the same blood and the Great Spirit is our Maker!"

The last word was only a whisper, barely understood, and then there was no more. When Crazy Horse felt the body stiffen his throat broke loose with a great sob and he flung himself beside his dead friend. "My brother, my brother!" he said brokenly. "Why do they always kill the best?"

Chapter 7

Little wars and bad luck

There was war with the whites now, but not quite the big thing Crazy Horse and Worm and Hump had thought would come. It was a kind of curling around the edges of the Lakota country, a probing and a feinting and a fending like two opponents unsure of themselves. The whites were tired after their big war, and many of their soldiers deserted when told they were to be sent against the Indians. Several attempts were made by the Indians to lure the soldiers into traps, at Julesburg and at the place called the Platte Bridge where the Holy Road and its wagon trains came across the river near a range of high hills, but too often the young and foolish warriors, anxious to get at the enemy, broke through the ranks of Akicitas and attacked too soon, giving the soldiers time to escape. Hump and Crazy Horse and other leaders were furious at them, but the warriors seemed to learn very slowly that strict discipline was necessary in this bitter war. Perhaps the biggest thing that happened was the rescuing of several dozen Indian families that were being marched east from Laramie by the soldiers toward the forts, to be herded and guarded like tame cattle. At Horse Creek the free Indians came in the dawn, gave guns to some of the captured ones, killed the little soldier chief and several of his soldiers, and got the captives away into the northern hills.

It was a time of great roving camps, the Lakotas, Cheyennes, and Arapahoes coming together like angry wasps after their nests have been disturbed, and sending out war parties on all sides to attack forts and wagon trains and isolated ranches. In the camps the great drums beat like the voices of the Thunder Beings, and the warriors rhythmically vowed with their strong brown bodies a total dedication to keeping alive the heartbeats of their nations—shaking their ankle rattles and waving their head feathers, stamping their feet until the ground shook and going as long as the drum went and past the time lesser men would have collapsed. Total mind, spirit, and body involvement are required in the ancient sacred dances and ceremonies of the peoples.

Many of the white soldiers seemed not to want to fight, and one great column of them in the north country, three thousand strong (Connor's column), was driven out of the country, not so much a result of fighting as of Lakota successes in stealing their horses and stock, and keeping them so tied down defending their camps that they returned on foot, exhausted and starving back to the east.

It was at Platte Bridge that a sad thing happened, for here the Oglalas saw their young friend, Casper Collins, now a little soldier chief, riding toward them through an assemblage of Cheyenne warriors, shouting *"Hou, Kola!"* And they let him through their ranks to protect a friend, but he chased down the road to try to rescue one of his men and was caught up again by a cluster of Cheyennes, wild to revenge Black Kettle and the Sand Creek Massacre, so that he went hopelessly down under their lances.

"Another good one gone of the very few the Wasichus have sent us!" mourned Crazy Horse to Hump, and the older warrior bowed his head and struck his heart, for he too had loved the brave young man. And Crazy Horse remembered another brave one, Bear Boy, and his eyes misted so that for a moment he could not see clearly in the fight.

Worm and his wife were worried about their two sons—Little Hawk, so reckless that it seemed that any girl who married him would soon be a widow, and young Crazy Horse, who had disappointed his parents by not courting through to marriage with the pretty younger sister of Yellow Woman, the Cheyenne he had saved after the massacre at the Blue Water.

"He is looking too long again at Black Buffalo Woman," said the mother. "He too often visits the Bad Face camp and the two talk together almost as if they were man and wife. He has

forgotten his great dream, and even our people
are only half in his mind."

The father bowed his head in thought. "It is
true there is something bad about this, and I
do not know where the trail leads, so that I am
afraid for him. I hope that soon he will find
another girl and leave alone the wife of No
Water, or there may be blood at the end."

Then came the time of the great ceremony
to select the shirt wearers, the assistants to
the chiefs, doing everything as in the long-ago
before the Oglalas lost their unity because of
the broken promises of broken treaties, the
hunger and disease, the whisky and the crazy
fighting between the Lakota warriors at the
forts and the traders' places. It was an old-time
custom nearly forgotten, but taken up again to
try to bring unity and strength to the people.
First there were four shirt wearers selected to
help the seven old man chiefs, called the Big
Bellies. And when the beautiful shirts made of
mountain sheep skins were held out in the great
council tipi, many gasped to see that the shirt
with the most tassels, each counting a brave or
good deed, was given to young Crazy Horse, he
who alone of all the others hid his head in shyness and acted as if he did not want this honor.
Of the other three, Young Man Afraid, son of
the great chief Man Afraid, accepted his shirt
as something due him because of his great family, while Sword, son of Brave Bear, the
Oykhpe chief, looked with thankfulness and
respect at the seven who had given this honor,
and American Horse, son of Sitting Bear of the
True Oglalas, could hardly keep his face from

bursting with pride as he sat up very tall and straight.

Worm and his wife, proud though they were, hoped that their son would listen to the old men who told the shirt wearers they must be worthy of this great honor and these sacred shirts by guarding the people from all harm and treating all with the greatest honor, even those who spoke or acted against them.

"I hope now he will stay away from Black Buffalo Woman," she whispered, with a mother's instinct.

But both parents forgot these forebodings as they heard the joyous trilling of the women, and the shouts of the warriors at this choice of four fine young men. And the people's spirit seemed to rise like a great wave, so that on that day all the Oglala acted as if they were one people. But some noted that Woman's Dress, son of Bad Face, moved away from the great lodge with a face dark as the thunder clouds, for he had hoped that the power of his father and of Red Cloud would get him a sacred shirt. Even later, when two other shirt wearers were named, Big Road and He Dog, Woman's Dress was again not mentioned. Crazy Horse was especially happy for He Dog, his boyhood friend, and he felt the two would have much to do with each other and in the fighting in the years ahead.

Other bad things besides war and buffalo killing came from the Wasichus. There was the spotted sickness and coughing diseases that hit especially the weak ones, the children, so that many died in the cruel winter of 1865–66, when the snows bound the land more than usual and no warm chinook wind came to break the ice early on the medicine waters. It was in this winter that Spotted Tail, Crazy Horse's mother's brother, the great Brulé chief, took his favorite daughter on the road to Fort Laramie to see if a doctor could heal her, but the girl died on the way and some of the heart and spirit went out of the Great Man on those last miles to the fort, walking with bowed head beside the dead body. Crazy Horse, remembering her pretty face and bright eyes and flashing smile the previous spring, felt the darkness of the world that came up to the Lakota from the Holy Road of the Wasichus, and made a man want to beat his fists against the ground.

And perhaps because he was sad over the death of this and other young ones of the Lakota and wished he had a young one of his own, born in love to see a better day and perhaps to help to herald it in, perhaps because of all this he came again and again to the camp of the Bad Faces, in the shadow of the lodge of Red Cloud, to be able to talk to Black Buffalo Woman, even though the women were now gossiping and No Water was a disapproving shadow in the background. But her clear eyes answered his and her voice was strong with feeling. He could not understand why he had lost this one whom he had teased into smiling and laughing with the tip of a feather so long ago when she was a baby. Had she not, by look and murmur, promised herself to him inside the blanket long before No Water came between them? Had he not proven his worth in painful patience, his dedication to the people in sacrificing and in battle? Was it not Lakota custom that a married woman had the right to leave one she did not love, and had many not done so, their husbands respecting the rights and the feelings of their wives?

In the winter of 1866–67 came the Battle of the Hundred Slain, the fight the Wasichus called the Fetterman Massacre; a good winter to be warm in the tipis, for it was the coldest even the old ones had seen. In the beginning of the Moon of Popping Trees, Crazy Horse felt the strange thing come again that was part of his growing medicine, the warmth surrounding him even on a cold day, as if the heat were blowing out from his body and driving away the cold so that the snow flakes did not touch him. It was like the feel he had for bullets and arrows, ghostly streaks coming through the air that he could dodge with a twist of the body before they could strike him, knowing exactly where they were coming.

Late in that moon the combined tribes of the Oglalas, Minneconjous, some Brulés, Cheyennes, and a few Blue Clouds or Arapahoes made a decoy and a trap outside Fort Phil Kearny at the headwaters of the Powder River. As usual, Crazy Horse led the decoys, pretending to attack the fort and then running away when the soldiers boiled out in answer to the three shots for help that came from their wood-gathering detail. It looked like a hundred soldiers coming out of the fort to save the wood-gatherers, and he knew that the little soldier chief who led them was Captain Fetterman, the one who had boasted he could take fifty men and ride through the whole Lakota nation. Let him come now and see what he could do! The decoys retreated and the soldiers followed them, coming faster and faster until Crazy Horse had to whip his horse down over the Lodge Trail Ridge and into the little canyon of the Peno where the warriors waited.

When both the riding and walking soldiers had rushed into the trap, Crazy Horse signaled his decoys to criss-cross their trails, and the warriors, seeing the sign from their hiding places, came rushing out of the brush and trees with a great shouting. Crazy Horse was in the thick of it from then on, hearing the whine of bullets and the swish of arrows, the white soldiers backing up and backing up, as their numbers fell, trying to find a place to make a stand, some brave men among them fighting valiantly on the edges to protect their brothers and going down under the clubs and arrows and bullets. A Minneconjou was the first to charge right through the main clump of whites, counting coup and clubbing as he went, and Crazy Horse followed, the wild cries around him like a great roar mixed with the screams of wounded horses and men.

Then all the soldiers were down except for a last group of cavalrymen who had let their horses go so they could climb quickly up behind some rocks on top of a little icy hill. Now the warriors crept over the ground toward them, their breath and even their hot bodies steaming in the cold. *"Hoppo! Ho! Up!"* shouted Hump and Crazy Horse when the time was right, and up the warriors rose in a wave that engulfed the last soldiers in a final flash of flame and smoke, the good back-loading rifles of these last ones shooting fast, but not enough to stop that charge. Then there were only the final deaths, the groans and deep sighing of wounded Indians, and the wind that told of a blizzard coming, whining in the leaves of the pines.

"So should it be for all those who come into our lands to take them away!" said Crazy Horse, and the warriors nodded.

The new grass and the warm sun came late that spring of 1867, and there was not much fighting for a while. But in the beginning of the Moon of Cherries Black, the Lakotas and their allies had a taste of future difficulties with back-loading guns when the wood-gatherers from Fort Phil Kearny were surrounded in a wagon-box fort they had made on the hill and stood off repeated charges of the warriors with their repeating rifles.

"We need those guns," growled Hump to Crazy Horse, "or they will slaughter us like the buffalo!"

In the Moon of Calves Growing Black Hair, Black Buffalo Woman had her third baby, but the gossips talked when Crazy Horse came often visiting to the village of the Bad Faces, and brought the elk teeth he had got from a herd the previous winter to make into neck-laces for her already abundantly laden woman's buckskins. In the camp of the Hunkpatilas, the mother of Crazy Horse told her husband, "No good will come of this love for a married woman. It is not our son of the great dream who does this, but one trapped by a girl's glances like a love-sick youth."

In the new year, at the end of the Moon of Snow Blindness, when the new green grass was soon to break through the hoar frost and the great bulls of the elk herds had ended their bellowing and were seeking spring yards, Crazy Horse, his brother Little Hawk, Little Big Man, and American Horse, led out a war party when they heard about a Lakota killed by a soldier down at one of the trading posts along the Holy Road. American Horse and his friends knew the owners of the Horseshoe Ranch along that road, and suggested they stop for a visit and to get a little powder. When they were met by bullets instead of friendship, the warriors circled the ranch house and fired the stables and the stockade, keeping the ones inside away from water. Twice the Lakota went away and twice they came back, finally firing the main house itself. On the second morning they found that all had burned down, but the whites had escaped through a secret tunnel to an outbuilding, got to a nearby ranch where there were horses, and taken off down the Holy Road toward Laramie.

With a whoop the Lakota war party was after them, Little Big Man noisiest of all and Little Hawk riding the most recklessly. Soon they had them partly cornered on a pine-tipped hill, and in the fight that followed, one by one was killed, including a man who bravely pulled an arrow out of his eye. Finally there were only four left, and these four stood stalwart, ready to die.

Suddenly Crazy Horse looked at the sky and saw the great Circle of All That Is, the earth forming its circle too, and the white-throated swifts making smaller circles high in the blue. And he realized that the whites too were men, children of the Great Spirit, and there were some among them good and brave. He remembered also Bear Boy and young Casper, who had died senselessly because someone had given him an untamed horse. So he rushed his horse forward just as Little Big Man was about to pull the trigger on his gun, and called out: "Enough! These are brave men. We will let them live."

"No! No!" Little Big Man shouted. "Do not all Wasichus wish our land? Let me kill!" But he flinched under the pale and angry glance of Crazy Horse and slowly lowered his gun, though his cheeks remained very dark.

Now Crazy Horse put down his knife and gun and walked toward the four with his hands uplifted in the peace sign. They held their guns on him, but he sat down in front of them without a sign of fear, took out his pipe from its case, stuffed it with tobacco, lit it, and smoked to the seven directions, while the bloody, tired faces in front of him gradually relaxed, and they too took the pipe in the age-old sign.

"Enough brave men have died," he said, and made slow sign talk that said: "We can be brothers, one day, white and red. Let us smoke to that day."

So he let them go free, after they had agreed to give some of their supplies to the Lakotas. But he knew he would need to watch Little Big Man

for a few days or there would be four scalps
in that one's pouch!

Now the Wasichus, in the Moon of Tender
Grass, were offering peace that many said was
a good thing, saying all the land from the Missouri to the white peaks of the Bighorns would
belong to the Lakotas and the Cheyennes,
including the Black Hills and all the Powder
River Country, as long as grass shall grow and
water flow. Even Man Afraid went down to
sign the papers, with Spotted Tail of the
Brulés, as also did Little Wound and many
other chiefs. But Crazy Horse and Worm said,
"Why sign for something we have always
owned?" And Red Cloud and Red Dog stayed
on the buffalo ranges and did not sign, nor did
Four Horns of the North, Sitting Bull, and
Black Moon of the Hunkpapas. Only after the
soldiers left the Powder River Trail, the forts
empty and silent under the warming sun of the
Moon of Shedding Ponies, did Red Cloud go to
the fort of the Wasichus to sign that treaty that
was to last forever, and give the red man a last-
ing haven of his own.

"How easily they forget," Crazy Horse said to
Worm. "Have we not seen what has happened
to the other Indians who signed such treaties?
Where today are their lands?" But the bulk of
the people heaved a sigh of relief. They were
glad to have peace, glad to have the traders
come with blankets and beads and guns, and
some of the soft and sweet white man's food
that the children liked so much. Glad were they
also to have the soldiers gone back to the east.

But it was not long before the people began to see that the peace was not as good as many thought. Soldiers kept the traders away from going to the Indians, and those traders that did get through were too often the whisky-peddlers who made the young Lakota men wild enough to do crazy things and even kill other Lakota. And the buffalo hunters were not only wiping out the herds to the south, but sneaking into the Lakota country every chance they had to get at the northern herds, using their many-shooting guns to hold off Lakota war parties that tried to stop them. So, even in the time of peace, the wasting away of wildlife and the power of the people was going on. To make things worse, there were quarrels between and within families as to whether to go in to be loafers about the forts, or to choose the old roving life of the high plains; some quarreling coming close to killing and breaking up families.

"The circle of our people is broken," mourned Worm, and his son, seeing the number of those who wanted the old way dwindling as the lure of the white man's way increased, had to nod in agreement.

But the thing that drove Crazy Horse furiously into the hills to think alone in the Silence was the coming of two Bad Faces to the Hunkpatila camp to warn Worm that his son must have nothing more to do with Black Buffalo Woman or there would be blood on the trail. "A woman of our people has the right to choose another for a mate if the first has proven wrong," he told his father. But the older man shook his head.

"There is too much power where her feet walk," he replied. "There is Black Twin, brother of No Water, who is strong as a shirt wearer, and others who are powers among the Bad Faces, including Red Cloud himself, who are against this thing. Think well, my son, about the women and children who will suffer if there is more blood spilled among the Oglala!"

Crazy Horse listened reluctantly, and noticed the bowed head of his mother, whom he also knew felt Black Buffalo Woman was no longer the one for him. So for a while he tried to put aside from his mind those eyes that now always seemed to look toward him with longing. Yes, he thought, I must think of the little and the weak who would suffer if there is bad blood again.

But then came in the Moon of Shedding Ponies, of the year the whites called 1869, a great and successful expedition against the Crows, driving them back behind the Bighorn, laughing and mocking at them even at the gate of their agency where they ran to hide behind the soldiers. And from this trip many warriors came back, singing the praises of Crazy Horse and his powers, his wonderful way of leading in battle, far in the forefront of all the others, daring the Crows to kill him until they feared him worse than a whole war party. But most of all they sang of the way he rescued the wounded and carried them back to safety out of the cold breath of death, so that all who traveled in his party felt they would be protected by his power.

"Let all the peace chiefs go to Washington!" the young warriors cried. "Here we have the true Lakotas! *Hoye!*"

Crazy Horse felt his heart swell within him, and he knew the time had come to stand firm even before his father. Was it not time now that one who no longer loved her husband should come to the one whom she had promised herself to in the long-ago? It had been a long wait!

He must have his own lodge now, separate from his father, so he took a small lodge near the camp of the Bad Faces.

Joy rushed within him when a few nights later he heard the soft step of moccasins outside, heard the flap lifted and knew the sweet sage and woman scent of one he loved. She was against him then, closer than she had ever been, her heart fluttering, telling him in a rush that she had left word for No Water that he was no longer her husband (the simple divorce of the Lakota, in this case long in decision) and had left her three children with relatives. Now at last she could walk free with the one she loved.

He was ready to take her with him in the dawn on a small war-party with women along to go west to the Yellowstone in search of the Crows. Many warriors were eager to be with Crazy Horse now and he had found several friends to go. So she rode with him proudly that first day in the warm late Moon of Shedding Ponies, her flesh soft but firm as the new-growing plants and the earth steaming in the sun after a light night rain, her buckskin dress swishing lightly with the sway of the horse, red and blue beads sparkling in the sun.

He had forgotten his mother and father and even that Little Hawk was far to the south on a war party that he had asked Crazy Horse to go on. He had forgotten Hump who had asked: "Come north with me to join the Hunkpapa and the Minneconjou in a great strike against the Wasichu along the Missouri."

"No," he had said, "it is not time."

But Hump had growled deep in his throat, and Crazy Horse had heard him faintly say the forbidden words: "The woman always comes between men!" and he had known that his warrior father was speaking about Black Buffalo Woman of whom he had always disapproved.

But now on the Plains heading toward the Little Bighorn Crazy Horse had forgotten all this, for he was delighting to the nearness of one who now radiated not the shyness of youth, but the surer love of a knowing woman, and his heart was singing with the knowledge of her nearness like a cloud of light and joy. Why could not a man serve his people with the woman of his long search, the one he had loved since childhood, even though she had three children and had been married to another man? Many honored women of the Lakota were of the same past. The question of trouble was way in the back of his mind now, and he pushed it away, as he swept his gaze back to meet the reward in her eyes, and the knowledge that she was his at last, riding with him into the wind that sang softly like a love song out of the west.

So it is often with a man before the darkness comes. On the second night the little party met a camp of friends, including Little Big Man and Little Shield, brother of Crazy Horse's best friend, He Dog, who invited them to eat with them. They had started to dip their hands in the hot wasna stew and to put the food on bark plates, when a great shouting and other noise swept up to the tipi and the flap was torn back without further warning. Into the tent lurched No Water, swaying a little, his eyes red-hot as coals.

"Look at me! I have come!" he shouted, and pointed his revolver at Crazy Horse. The young Oglala jumped to his feet in a flash, drawing his knife, but Little Big Man grabbed his knife arm from behind and jerked it back just as No Water pulled the trigger. The crashing sound in the tent stunned everybody and Crazy Horse felt a ripping across his upper jaw, the flashing fire that comes just before unconsciousness, and he fell forward into the flames.

As Little Shield and Little Big Man hastily pulled him out of the heat, No Water turned blindly and ran from the tipi, laughing like one crazy. And those who had heard of the dream of Crazy Horse knew that just as in the dream, one of his own people had held his arm while another Oglala attacked him. And when the thought came that he was dead because he lay so still, the roar of the warriors rose like a great wind, the women trilling the call to victory, for suddenly there were those ready to kill for

Crazy Horse, and once again, as at the time of
Bull Bear, thirty years before, the Oglala were
cracking apart into two hostile camps.

"The Bad Faces, the Bad Faces!" some cried.
"They have always been jealous of our Strange
Man! It is time to kill!" Only Little Big Man was
silent, for the eyes that looked upon him were
dark with anger, and he slipped away to safety
as soon as he could.

But No Water and his friends were gone
when the warriors went looking for them, gone
on swift horses to the south, making few tracks
to follow because they rode in stream beds and
rocky places, so that the warriors gathered
themselves like a coiled spring, ready to go
against the Bad Face camp itself. By the next
day Worm had arrived and his brother, Long
Face, and Bad Heart Bull came, with face long
and sad, for it was he, he admitted, who had
loaned the pistol to No Water to go hunting
with, something he would never have done if
he had known the true purpose. But No Water
had seemed gay and friendly, with no hint of
the darkness in his heart.

Then these three looked at Crazy Horse, lying
still under the ministrations of the Medicine
Man, who had sewn up the wound and placed
warm compresses of healing herbs on it, saying
"He breathes and is alive; he will be well
again!"

For hours they watched like men made of
stone, but gradually the color began to come
into the pale face, the young Oglala moved a bit
and his eyes opened. He saw his father and the
other older men around him and he began

slowly and painfully to signal with his hands, being unable to talk.

"Let there be no war among our people because of me," the signs said. "Protect Black Buffalo Woman. She did no wrong."

So the old men called the warriors and talked to them quietly, telling them what Crazy Horse had said, and that he would live. Many made the deep growling in the throat that meant anger against No Water and other Bad Faces that had encouraged this thing, but finally all agreed to follow the wishes of Crazy Horse. Yet many knew there would be bad blood among the Oglala for many a day.

Crazy Horse had been moved a few miles away to the lodge of another uncle of his, Spotted Crow, where his mother and father also came to help him heal by their presence and the food his mother made for him when he could eat. And here he heard that Black Buffalo Woman had first been taken to the lodge of Bad Heart Bull and then finally back to the lodge of No Water where the warning was given that she was not to be harmed. And there she took up her woman's work again and gathered her three children around her. And all knew she would not belong to Crazy Horse beyond that short time they had been allowed.

So Crazy Horse now swallowed this bitter medicine, for he was blaming himself for coming near to destroying the unity of his people in this time when they were being attacked from every direction. Matters became worse for him when he learned that Little Hawk, his reckless younger brother, had not come back from the south where he had gone in a war party against the whites. One came from the south who was badly frightened because he said the white miners, the freighters, and the Gray Men (bandits) had formed a secret society to kill Indians. He feared they had gotten Little Hawk.

When Crazy Horse was well enough to use a gun again, though weak, they took him with a party north of the Yellowstone to hunt buffalo, and it was in this place under the blue sky and with the murmur of great waters that he heard at last from the war party of Little Hawk. The survivors came sadly into the camp one day and told how Little Hawk had been in a fight with the bad Wasichus who had sworn to kill Indians, how they had all raced their horses to get away from the hail of bullets, but found that Little Hawk was no longer with them. They went back to look for him and found him lying on the wet ground at a place where he had charged the party of whites in his reckless way alone.

They looked at Crazy Horse and saw his face darken as no man had seen it darken before, and they thought he was angry at them, and shrank before him, but he called them back with a voice that shook: "I am responsible for this and no other! He asked me to go with him, but I refused because I thought only of the woman!" And he turned his head away so none could see his eyes, and all quietly left the tipi. But when his mother returned later to prepare the food for dinner, he cried to her from his heart's depths: "*Why?*"

She said quietly, "You must understand that

the Great Being did not want you to have this woman for a wife, for she turned away from you at the one moment when it counted, when she had to stand up and say her love for you was greater than the power of her relatives."

She paused now, and her eyes looked beyond the dinner she was preparing and beyond the tipi and beyond the camp circle. "Perhaps in another time such a one as she will be strong enough to choose and to be wife to an Itanca with great visions. And perhaps in another time men such as No Water and families such as hers will look beyond personal loss to the place in destiny of those they are close to. Perhaps another in another day, with your spirit, will be given one as beloved as Black Buffalo Woman who will in that time, also a time of great need, bear the children that have your spirit and your vision and can lead our people."

He nodded slowly, showing he understood the demands of the times in which he lived, and drew his hand through his hair, then said only quietly to himself: I must think of my people first.

And as if she read his mind she said quietly: "In the wild places you will have the dreams that tell you what to do."

But the new way for Crazy Horse was not to start until one more act born of a depth of feeling beyond common feeling would shake him. Learning that one he had seen riding nearby on a golden buckskin was No Water, he leaped bareback on a fast gelding and took off in the direction he had gone. When he got near him, No Water began to quirt the buckskin frantically, and they raced over the waves of the grass until No Water reached the Yellowstone and plunged into the swirling waters. His horse was strong and bore him to safety, but Crazy Horse stood on the bank with his gun in hand and did not fire it. He knew that No Water would never come back again to a camp of the Oglalas that was near that of the Hunkpatilas.

He knew also that there might be trouble from this act of his, and it happened when there was a meeting of the Big Bellies, the old men chiefs, and all but one of them, Man Afraid, were against him now because of the power of Black Twin and Red Cloud.

They said Crazy Horse had broken the rules of the shirt wearers by chasing No Water after No Water had sent horses to make up for the shooting. Fourteen armed men were sent to the lodge of Crazy Horse to ask that the Sacred Shirt be given back, but Man Afraid came along to see that there was no fighting.

Weeping, the mother of Crazy Horse went at his bidding and got the shirt, beautiful in its beads and fringed mountain sheepskin, to give to the men to take back to the Big Bellies, where Man Afraid shamed them all by standing up and saying loudly: "I have seen some very bad work tonight! No other man shall wear this shirt, for none will be worthy of it."

Chapter 8

The great vision

It was 1871, a year of pause and peace in the Lakota Country, when Crazy Horse went up alone to Bear Butte, the sacred mountain of both the Lakota and the Cheyennes, for a vision search. He chose the first half of the Moon of Making Fat, when the whole warm earth was waving green under grass made thick by the rain from the Thunder Beings, when the young antelope were playing among the hills, and the buffalo herds were like black earth clouds along the Powder and the edges of the Paha Sapa, the Black Hills. He wanted it to be so, at the height of all the good things of the earth and sky, the bobolinks and meadowlarks trilling from bush and grass clump, the prairie dogs whistling their alarm when his horse came prancing past their clusters of holes and mounds, the swallows hissing through the air by his head, the grasshoppers and butterflies flashing red, yellow, orange, and blue wings everywhere, and the warm, warm earth and leaf smell rising up like a heady perfume.

He was leaving a good warm lodge behind him too when he came, not the home of his mother and father any more, but his own lodge and his own woman, Black Shawl, one whom He Dog and Spotted Crow and others of his good friends had found for him in Big Foot's band. She was prettier than he had expected, but what was much better was the soft, quiet way she had taken control of his lodge, her voice like rippling waters, the least touch of her hands filled with kindness and love. Yet they were hands used to hard work, the fletching of skins, the cutting up of meat, the carrying of buffalo stomachs filled with water from the nearest springs or creeks, the endless sewing of buckskin clothes and rents in the wall of the tipi.

It was a new experience for the lonely man to see one seated opposite him at the cooking fire, day after day, while smelling the good food preparing, and seeing her look at him with that liquid, dark look so like and yet so stirringly different from the look of a mother. It was good also to feel that there would be no trouble over this one, for she came free of any jealous husband, and a sense of peace and all-goodness flowed through that lodge. And now, as he rode toward the mountain, he knew there was another life stirring within this new wife, soon to be a son or daughter.

There was another sense of goodness coming with him also, for he had become indeed Itanca, leader in the Indian way, one who watched over the camp as a mother prairie hen watches over her children—one who had become the protector, as the bull buffalo stations himself between the herd and danger. He experienced a wonderful pleasure in coming into the camp in the dawn or early evening, so quiet and shadowlike that even the camp dogs failed to notice him, bringing meat to a lodge where there was a widow or where the man was too wounded or sick to go hunting. And the herds of horses he ran down or captured from the enemy Crows or Pawnees melted away like the snow in the Moon of Tender Grass, because he always made sure that each family had an extra horse to pull travois with or one to carry an old woman or man when the trail was long and tiring between camps. So the glances that followed him from men and women and children were filled with a mixture of love and awe and wonder, like the lakes mirroring back the warmth and light of the sun.

Yet there was a strange and terrible uneasiness that drove him to go alone to the top of Bear Butte for a Hanblecheyapi, a vision search. Behind all the good things that had recently happened to him, back of the peace and warmth of the lodge and camp circles, the Wasichus hovered beyond the great circle of the horizon like the ominous gray cloud of a coming blizzard in the Moon of Frosting in the Lodge. The cold of this feeling struck into his heart even on this warm summer day, and he tried to lift it off and gather hope from the beautiful things of earth and sky that surrounded him.

"Crying for a Vision," the Hanblecheyapi means in the Lakota language, and the heart of Crazy Horse was indeed crying to the Great Spirit, asking: "Why have they come, these people who destroy the earth and its life, who take the beautiful world away from the Indians and make it into a senseless place where the true things of the Spirit are forgotten because they put gold and the things it will buy first? What can we do to stop them?"

He remembered the tales he had heard of what had happened to the Santee Lakota to the east, to the Mandans, the Sacs and Fox, and the Iowas and Pottawottami. They dwelt now on little reservations in shacks of wood, not the proud tipis or birchbark houses of old. There they were servants of the white men, looked down upon and given cast-off clothes, while the terrible bottles of whisky and wine dragged them lower like a dark hand clutching the heart out of them, dulling the senses. Was this now to come to the Teton Lakota, a proud people who would also be beaten down by the endless waves of whites until the spirit was gone and they were a folk like death?

He shivered as he thought these dark thoughts and remembered then his father's words: "My son, when you go to the mountaintop to pray, cast aside from your mind all thoughts save thoughts of the Great Spirit, of beauty and of strength. Call on Him for help for your people and for yourself so you can help your people. Purify the very breath you breathe with thoughts of the spirit until your thoughts rise like the eagles into the sky, up

and up to be one with the Sun and the One
Who is Behind the Sun. Be humble as the earth
before all things, and when you have left the
voices the body listens to, let the Spirit of Being
flow into you until the secret Voice whispers to
you through the needles of the pines the meaning of your life and what is to be."

So he drove the darkness from his soul as the
great bear drives the wolves from the carcass
of the elk he has killed, and he galloped his
horse to the last level spot on the side of the
mountain where a little stream tinkled down
over the rocks and a cluster of cottonwood
trees hid a small vale filled with lush grass like
a jewel, where the horse could be hobbled
safely out of sight from a war party far below.
Leaving his horse here, he took with him up the
steep slope only his sacred pipe, a buffalo skin
robe, some tobacco, a little food to be offered
to the spirits, a bundle of the sacred sagebrush,
four wild cherry sticks, and four small banners
of yellow, red, black, and white to tie to the
sticks that represented the four sacred directions.

The climb up Bear Butte was like climbing
a ladder up into the sky, there being places
where the rocks formed steps amidst the pines.
He knew he was going to a spot where few
other men had ever dared to go for a Hanblecheyapi, a place so sacred and so dangerous it
was whispered that lightning from the Thunder Beings had struck down those who dared
to stay there, so that most vision seekers made
their quests somewhere on the safer slopes
below. When he reached the top, the glory of

the earth was spread beneath, the waves of
emerald green grass rolling to the east and
north and south as far as eye could see, while
to the southwest the great dark bear humps of
the Paha Sapa filled the edge of the sky like dark
thunderheads. Here the wind was blowing a
little song through the pine needles and a few
ants and beetles were crawling over the rocks
about his feet. It was as if he were alone at the
center of the world, and his heart swelled as he
turned to see the lovely green earth far below
and the sacred circle of the sky coming down
to meet the sacred circle of the earth. Here, if
anywhere in the world, he thought, the Great
Spirit can come to speak to a man who is a true
seeker. Here, maybe, the white-throated swift,
dodging over the rocky crest of the bluff like a
sweeping spot of light, would carry his cry to
the Above One and bring him back an answer
for his people.

He made a circle about himself of the sacred
pipe tobacco, made mainly of the leaves of the
red willow and kinnikinnick, spread his sagebrush over the sharp rocks for a bed, and placed
his yellow-, red-, white-, and black-bannered
prayer sticks of wild cherry wood pointing to
the four directions. The food and his loin cloth
were placed outside the circle, but the buffalo
robe lay beside the sagebrush for use when the
cold winds of night would come. Next he took
hold of the bowl of his pipe in his right hand
and pointed the stem to the west, crying the
sacred song: *"Wakan Tanka onshimala ye oyate
wani wachin cha!"* (O Great Spirit, be merciful
to me that my people may live!)

Then he walked out to the sacred pole on the west and cried again the song, but here he added a variation of his own choosing, singing: "O Thou where the sun goes down, send me courage that I may be always brave for my people and protect them in danger." Then he returned to the center again.

Next he pointed the stem to the north, crying the usual song, but out at the north pole he sang also: "O Thou Giant of the North, give me of Thy great strength that I may help my people."

To the east, besides the holy song, he sang: "O Thou where the sun rises, give me of Thy purity and wisdom, that I may be like the new snow and the fresh spring water in my heart, and that I may be wise like the great chiefs of old who led the people in the holy ways."

To the south, besides the holy song, he sang: "O Thou producer of green plants and all good growing things, help me to grow in the spirit until I can lead my people where they will be safe from the Wasichus."

Now he pointed his pipe stem down to the earth, and sang: "O Thou Mother Earth, make me humble as you are when the feet of men walk upon you, yet give me your power to grow in the spirit."

Next he pointed his pipe stem up to the sky, saying after the sacred song: "O Thou Who art the Center of All Things that Are; come to me in vision that I may know what to do for my people."

Last he swept the pipe stem around in a complete circle and pointed it once more to the sky, crying: "O Thou Sacred One, Wakan Tanka, I send my spirit up to Thee. Send it back to me that Thy power may be within me, not for me, but for my people."

Having thus sent his cry to the seven sacred directions, he was going to start all over at the beginning, as all the old ones did, but a sudden thought came to him, and he cried in a loud voice, so that a bluejay flying by suddenly swerved in fright: "O Thou Whose voice calls to me in the leaves of the pines, I have cried to you for the seven sacred circles, but tell me what is the meaning of the two circles yet to come?"

And he trembled for a minute in sudden fear, for he knew none of his people had asked this presumptuous question before. Then he gripped his pipe bowl hard once more, swung it to the west as he had done in the beginning, and started once more to make his motions toward the seven directions, and his songs. But at the end of the seven, as before, he asked his question about the eighth and ninth circles, and this time he was not afraid any more.

So the sun swung across the sky and down until it ebbed its great red disk below the horizon, and the cool shadows of the night wind began to whisper through the pines. Now Crazy Horse drew his warm buffalo robe around his body, and dropped down upon the fragrant sage to rest, but holding his mind like a crystal drop of dew poised on the tip of a leaf as he lay relaxed. Whenever he felt rested enough, he would rise up once more under the circle of brilliant stars, sending his call out to the constellations of the west, the north, the east, and the south, then down to Mother Earth and up to Father Sky and finally, drawing the Spirit in the seventh direction, into his inner being. At times the wind grew stronger and colder, whipping and tugging at his buffalo robe and sending its keening through the pine needles, but his mind remained always flowing outward with his spirit like a river that could never run empty, so that the warm blood touched his outer veins and arteries, keeping the skin warm.

When the dawn came it was first only a faint haze of light on the edge of blackness, then a growing ribbon of light around the rim of the world, then a dull red disk that touched the eastern edge of the vastness of the plains, then a sudden blazing glory that sent its vibrant colors across the sky and around the sacred circle of the meeting of earth and sky. And he knew, though he could not hear it yet, that the Great Spirit was talking to him out of the heart of the sky, the land, and the light. The waves of grass that stretched to the edge of earth flashed brilliant green below him, the sky turned a blue he had never seen before, and in its center he saw an eagle dropping earthward like a plunging meteor. So he was like a little child who waits patiently until his grandfather speaks again of a marvelous story. All things that existed in the universe were trembling on the edge of his mind like a flood about to tip over a cliff.

So he prayed and sang now with a rhythm that was the rhythm of earth and sky, of wave and wind and cloud, of summer and winter and

night and day, until all tiredness and hunger
and thirst left him as if they had never been.
Thus it went on through the hours that were
no longer counted, but were only a smooth running like the wind, until late on the third day
the great black thunderheads loomed to the
west of him, forming armies marching eastward, until the Thunder Beings were talking
above him in the darkening sky where the lightning flashed and flickered.

A shower of large hailstones came out of the
sky, and a bolt of lightning leaped from the
mountaintop only thirty feet from him, so that
the thunder nearly broke his eardrums in one
mighty clash, and then the hailstones were falling in myriads, but strangely none hit him or
near him, and he felt as if suspended in space
in the hands of the Great Spirit, so that he lay
down as one tired would lie down in a bed at
home after a hard day, but surrounded by
peace. The fragrance of the sage grew in his
nostrils until the odor was poignant with
memories, and he fell asleep remembering the
youth that had been Curly and the time the
first vision came to him as he lay in the sagebrush under the cottonwood tree of long ago.

Now a sparrow hawk was fluttering above
him, uttering its *killy-killy* cry, as they do when
they hover in the sky. And the cry turned into
words that pierced his mind like waves of light,
because there was no sound with them any
more, but he understood their meaning.

"*Look down!*" the voice said, "*and behold what
is to be!*"

So he found himself standing on the top of

Bear Butte in the sunlight, and his eyes were such that he could see very far away things in detail, as with the far-seeing glasses he once took from a fallen soldier. So he looked below and there was a town of the white people there, with many houses, and he saw them busy with their work like many ants, but he felt a coldness from them that he did not understand until he saw on the edge of this town some poor shacks where Indians lived. The Indians wore old cast-off white men's clothes and their eyes were sullen like the darkness of a cloud where the Thunder Beings talk. He saw two of them lying still in the middle of the street where water puddles were, and there was about them the stink of too much whisky. An Indian woman was washing clothes in a backyard, by rubbing them on a rough board with soap, but there was about her all the weariness of the world, as if she could hardly move another inch. And he felt so sorry for her that he wanted to go down from his place near the sky and do the work for her so she could rest. So he knew that the old spirit had gone from these people and a great sadness came over him that he could hardly bear, as if this sick thing was coming right into his heart. And he knew who had caused this thing to happen, and who had put the wall between peoples, holding one down while the others took whatever they wanted. So his anger flashed like the lightning and he wished he grasped a gun, or even a lance so he could plunge down to attack. To die to save his people from this would be good. But the voice out of the light spoke again. *"This had to be,"* it said. *"But it will pass away, for all the people of Earth must gather together like the geese that fly together in springtime. . . . Watch now, and be alert to see!"*

He seemed to be breathing deeply then, as if he were sucking in the wind of heaven and his heart grew calmer, so that when he looked again, he saw not only the broken hearts and minds below him among his people, but also the few strong ones who somehow kept the spirit through all the bad times. *For there were old men and women there whose faces mirrored the clouds and the earth, and whose eyes had the light of the dawn, and he could see that they were passing on this spark to some few of their grandchildren.*

Now as he looked below he saw that there were black ribbons across the prairies where before there had been only green grass, and going along these black ribbons were little many-colored bugs that moved with great speed. And when he looked closer, with his far-seeing eyes, he saw that there were white people and even a few Lakota traveling inside these strange swift bugs, and he saw that there were few horses any more.

Then the darkness all over the earth seemed to be increasing, but there were loud noises and whistlings and screams within it, and he sensed that most of the males of the earth were fighting one another. And he saw the emptiness and pain and tears in the faces of families, including Lakota families, and knew that somewhere their loved ones were being killed.

There was a time after this fighting when

people ran about like crazy and seemed to be accomplishing nothing except putting up more buildings. But he looked into the sky and saw that there was an increasing number of large things that looked like birds with wings, but were not birds, that were flying through the sky, and in the nighttime they had many little lights. Then again came a great darkness and again a feeling of the males of the earth fighting and dying, while the very air seemed to scream and the explosions were so great that they rocked the mountains and he saw a place of many houses disappear beneath a great smoke cloud as if it had never been.

Now there came a new time after the second great war, and he saw a new hope beginning to appear among the faces of his people, and some were gathering together for the dances in a new way, trying to keep the things that deaden the minds, the crazy water bottles and the drugs that destroy, away from these gatherings, so that here and there the surge of the spirit was so strong that some of the men were singing strong heart songs and the women were trilling as in the old days. They were wearing better clothes now and living in better houses, but he could see also that there were still too many little walls, and one great wall yet between them and most of the white people.

Suddenly all the people's faces disappeared, and he saw the whole world as if it were in darkness, but there was a dawn light coming from the east and before it the daybreak star approached through the sky. It was a star with nine points, and he knew these represented the nine sacred circles, including the two new ones yet to come. Then he saw the sacred herb beginning its climb out of the earth. It was eerie to see the fresh green rising from a place of death, for it grew where a dead tree had been and as the dawn began to turn the whole east to glorious light, the herb grew again into the Sacred Tree of his people, with the branches full of flowers and singing birds, and below the tree, spirit people and animals and birds were dancing and singing as if they had all the joy in the world but could not contain it.

Then, behind this world of glorious light, which he knew was the real world of the spirit, he saw the dark other world filled with people as if in a swamp or quicksand, but some beginning to reach their hands out toward the light, some seeing it and some not seeing it, as with men on the trail of a mountain lion, some seeing the little places where the paws bowed down a grass or herb and others not seeing these places at all, but only seeing the rocks and plants in a haze like one mass.

"Do you see it?" some people were saying to others. "Do you see that light coming? It is so wonderful!" But other people looked and shook their heads and their faces remained sad, or dull and ugly. They grimaced as a hermit does who has been shut in a cave of darkness for years and resents bright light which he is unable to deal with. Only slowly can his eyes and mind take in and understand any light.

The faces of the ones more ready were slowly turning to beauty and glory. *Then he saw that these people were already dancing in the spirit*

under the sacred tree, for the dawn of under-
standing was penetrating and they were ready.
There were many different faces under that
tree, so he understood that it was a tree too big
for just his people alone, but included all races
of all men, white and yellow, black and brown
or red. And their faces were full of laughter
and joy. And they formed one circle of one
people, united though different in a strange
and sacred way that he did not quite under-
stand.

When he awoke on the high top of Bear
Butte, it was early daylight and the sun had
just tipped the horizon to flood the earth with
light. Down the slope the rock wrens were singing as if their hearts would burst, chanting
their varied *"tu-tu-tu, chrr-ee, chrr-ee, chee-*
poo, chee-poo, chee-poo!" with such joy that it
seemed that what would be was now here.
Weak from fasting, he had been allowed the
gift of eternity. Time and space had dissolved.
Only as his consciousness returned to the times
of 1871 and the place on top of Bear Butte did
he realize the long and hard stages ahead until
the light would come.*

* The exact year of this vision is not known—1871
seems the most logical.

Chapter 9

It is hard to hold to a great vision

When Crazy Horse told his vision to his father, the older man smoked for a long time in silence. He thought of the other hill where they had sat together, long before. He thought of the doe whose son nearly outran her. The man he called son had been given a vision greater than any he would have. And the son's understanding might one day outreach that of the father. So it was more to himself that he at last spoke, and also because the son must discuss his vision, for a vision too long unshared becomes like a child too long in arriving. Worm knew as he spoke that one day his son might see the vision more clearly than he, but now he spoke. And now his son listened.

"There is both good and bad about this vision. The bad is that you saw our people conquered and living in the square gray houses that Drinks Water saw. You saw the crazy water hurting many, and you saw the Wasichus running the lives of the Lakota as if they were the spotted cattle. But you saw also that some still carried the great dreams in their secret hearts, and sang them when they were alone, so that not all our people became like the black ants when the red ants make them slaves. Out of the darkness the light of a new day finally came shining, and then these bearers of the secret helped spread that new light to all peoples.

"This I see we must do. We Lakota are the most powerful of the Plains tribes. We must try to make allies of other tribes and raise all our strength to stop the white men, even though, in the long run, we cannot win. We must because the story of our courage and our fighting will be sung down the years ahead to give heart to all the Indian peoples, for they will know our warriors died bravely and we will show that the Wasichu can be defeated. And there must be some among our leaders whose honor and courage stand out like shining stars in a dark night, keeping the spirit alive among the few until the New Time comes. Gather around you, my son, while there is still time, all the young people you can. Tell them the stories of the great dreams and the great heroes, and be yourself, while humble, one to whom they can look for guidance, one who speaks always with the straight tongue, one who is never afraid, and one who fights always for justice for his people regardless of what may happen to himself or what others may say."

Again Worm smoked and was silent, while his son bowed his head in deep thought. Then the old holy man spoke for the last time: "The great hope is that one day there will come to us white men and other peoples too, seeking the wisdom of our people, seeing the circle of earth and sky, seeing the hoop of all men under the Great Spirit. For a while we will not dare talk to most white people about these things, for they will laugh at us as the silly young jackrabbit laughs at the wise coyote, because he thinks that since he can run faster he can always escape.

"But your dream tells us there will come a time when more and more will see the wrongness of the ways of the Wasichus, even among their own people. More and more will see they are out of touch with the Great One above, even though they bow before him and say their prayers, and have buildings where they worship Him. More and more will see they have lost the circle and must find it again, and that the Indian peoples can help them, for we are of the earth and sky and some of us will never forget this. And when we help them, all men that are still alive after the times of trouble that must come will come together in One Circle and we will be one people, filled with the glory of the spirit. So did the vision of White Buffalo Calf Maiden promise us, and so also does your vision. Be brave then, my son, and take hope, even when the darkness comes, for does not the sun always rise again after even the darkest night, and does not the beautiful warmth of springtime come again with its flowers and singing birds even after the coldest winter?"

Crazy Horse had always been interested in the youth of his tribe, stopping to speak to them

with words of encouragement at their work or
games, and joining in telling them the great
stories of the people. But now he became far
more active than before at this, so that the
younger Black Elk, or Fire Thunder, and many
another boy, and sometimes girls too, would
come to his lodge, to sit in the sacred circle
with the firelight playing over the bronze faces
and the dark eyes both intent and shy. Though
his voice was quiet, it was also vibrant, and he
used his hands when he spoke as the eagle uses
his wings to signal to his mate, so that there
was something about those evenings around the
fire that was full of magic. The magic of the
great dreams and the great hero stories and
songs were woven by those moving hands and
that quiet voice until every eye was gleaming
and the dark sinewy hands of the listeners
tensed in the firelight like warriors awaiting an
overdue signal.

Back in the shadows Black Shawl was a presence, calm and adoring, her eyes watching her
husband, intense as any youth, but her hands
busy when the time came to pass hot tea or
coffee, and the good cooked meat.

The time came also when she was absent for
a little while from the camp circle, coming
back with a new voice that cried to the earth
and sky until the gentle crooning soothed it, for
to Crazy Horse a girl child had been born. And
this girl indeed became the very life of his
heart, for she grew to be a sweet child with
pale brown curling hair like her father in his
youth, and the far-seeing eyes. In those eyes
were the meaning of her name which her

father gave her, saying she would walk in sacred ways. She grew big enough to love to ride on his back and kick his ribs as if he were her horse, and laugh with a delight that sent his heart to racing. But, as she grew a little older, he saw both the tiny girl and Black Shawl coughing with the white man's disease that eats the lungs, and a dark shadow was over him then with every passing day. "Even from afar," he thought, "the Wasichus send their poison among us so that our helpless ones might die." So he looked at the little one, she whom he had called "They Are Afraid of Her," and those who saw, saw also the tearing apart of this man by the times in which he lived.

Yes, and it was a bad time for the people too, with storms of disagreement rising between those who wished to live near the white men and be given food, and those who still sought the free way of old, the life with dignity. The old chiefs' society was long gone now, for those men, faced by the hunger of their people and the closing-in horizon, had taken what they considered the lesser of two bad choices and had moved into the agencies to fight for the doles of food and clothing the agent gave them. "Like coyotes coming to the left-over food of wolves," said Worm.

But worst of all was the shrinking of the buffalo herds, growing less and less numerous so fast that the headmen and the medicine men spent many nights talking over what could be done.

"It is coming true!" the wise ones muttered. "Drinks Water long ago told our grandfathers that the strangers from the east would drive our friends, the buffalo, into the earth, and all the other animals with them!"

But Crazy Horse was gathering slowly a nucleus of fighting men around him, drawn in by the tales of his bravery in battle and by the way the bullets never hit him, by his ability in avoiding the Wasichus who sought him, by the way he saved the wounded ones, and by his wisdom. So one by one young men came away from the agencies to join him, to be with one who preferred the life of the plains, hard though it was to find food, preferring it to the tame way where the Wasichus ruled. He taught them to search for visions with the Hanbleche-yapi, to find help from the powers of the universe, and he taught them a new tactic against the armies of the Wasichus.

"We have been fighting the Wasichus in the old way of the Plains tribes, to count coup by touching the enemy though not necessarily killing him." Disliking the very words that must come from his mouth, he continued. "In this day, what was once honorable now must be changed in order that our people live. We too must now fight to kill. And we must not fear as our ancestors did not fear what must be done, so we can move very swiftly to the attack, but dodging while we run or ride so we are hard to hit. If you pray for the power, you may be told by feeling where the bullet is coming, how to get out of the way in time. We must divide into two groups and practice, one pretending to be Wasichus firing, the others Lakotas charging. If you practice this sudden charging from behind shelter until it becomes part of your thinking, then you will do this without fear and the sudden swift attack will cause the enemy to fire wildly and so miss us. Also we waste time taking scalps. The Wasichus fight to kill and they only take scalps if they are sure they have won and have plenty of time."

So they practiced hour after hour, both on horse and on foot, until they moved as one man, and Crazy Horse taught them special signals by whistle and arm that they learned to obey instantly.

"So do we move as one," he told them, "and yet each alone in a way to strike the enemy with fear and to hold the trigger finger, for we have few bullets ourselves and they must be used wisely."

"*Hoh!*" shouted the young warriors, and they made the sign of unity, the hoop against the sky, feeling now that under Crazy Horse there would be more hope against the whites who had spent centuries building unlimited war machines while the Lakota had been building spiritual union with All That Is. And Crazy Horse looked at them and their eager eyes and was heartened, but deep within he knew many a brave one would die.

Then he came home one day with a war party that had been against the Crow, one of the battles of survival in the clash for the few remaining buffalo ranges. He knew when he saw the camp of his people that a bad death had come. His heart seemed to move to his throat when he drew near and saw the torn clothing, the blood drying on the arms of the ones who had offered the sacrifice of their flesh, their most personal gift, in sympathy, all women, their faces broken with mourning.

"Be strong, my son," said Worm when father and son met. And slowly the father and mother told him how the coughing disease that came from the Wasichus had weakened "They Are Afraid of Her" until at last the final spark of life left the little girl that was his daughter. He knew they did not want him to go, but he had to see her even in death and he rode away across the prairies, hunting for where they told him the burial scaffold rose toward the sky. And, for a while as he rode, a terrible rage followed the blood through his body, causing his hands to clench until the nails bit into the flesh, and he wished he could kill all the Wasichus who, uninvited, visited their darkness upon his people. When he saw the scaffold, the little bundle, the beloved buckskin doll tied tight against it, and the rattle and other toys, his father's heart broke as does a great flood when the Thunder Beings fill the sky with rain and the deep beat of their drums. He flung himself on the ground and wept until all life seemed as empty as a broken gourd or a prairie chicken egg the ants have sucked dry.

A day and a night and another day passed while he lay there, but at last the blood of life moved through his veins again and he knew the call of his people came to him over the far hills. "They Are Afraid of Her" would be out of reach of his arms, but there was still a great task to do. So he rose as does a wounded bear, but the wound within him was deeper than any wound of the flesh and would take longer to heal.

He came home to the bad news that Custer and a thousand soldiers and civilians, plus fifty Indian scouts, had been to the Black Hills and had found gold. Worse still was the news that the Lakota had been so short of ammunition they had not dared to attack the long army train, and Custer had come out scot-free from his invasion of Indian lands without permission. "Gold and Custer in the sacred Paha Sapa!" exclaimed Crazy Horse. "The chiefs are mad to let him get away with this! Now the Wasichus are sure to come like a great flood!"

Far off in the agencies the young warriors seemed to hear his cry that hot summer of 1874, and many came to join him. But it was too late. Already Custer and his troops had escaped back to safety. But in the Moon of Colored Leaves and the Moon of Falling Leaves he led war parties into the Black Hills, the Sacred Paha Sapa, and they came back with pack loads of food and ammunition and many white men's guns that had belonged to miners foolishly after gold, in land that by treaty belonged to the Indians "as long as rivers ran and grass did grow."

In the Moon of Popping Trees and the Moon of Frosting in the Lodge, the word came to the Crazy Horse camp that the loafers at the forts were dying of cold or starving because of poor or moldy or no food, of only one blanket given to three or four Indians, until the ones holding out in the north and west had to come in and share skins and robes with their brothers, even those who were trying the white man's way. It was cold and blizzardy that winter, with poor hunting even in the west, so there was little choice sometimes between begging for the food of the Wasichus and hunting for the few remaining buffalo and elk. Many were praying in the old holy way for times to change, but it seemed that the prayers were not answered, and Crazy Horse remembered his vision of the dark days that were to come before there would be light again.

But he heard with dark anger of the herds of cattle driven north and west to feed the Indians at the agencies, and how half or more of the animals were stolen or sold along the way so that the pitiful herds that finally arrived were hardly enough to keep a small band alive. And what of the little ones and the sick, he thought, hearing also of the many new crosses made on the bluffs where the burial parties dug every day that winter. Then worst of all the word came that the Wasichus were saying they wanted to buy the Black Hills, and the uglier hidden word that if they were not sold them, they would take them anyway with the army. So again the words of white men and the papers they wrote on were nothing but lies, and the Lakotas knew that many were laughing behind their hands at how the Indians had been tricked. So was the sacred circle being broken, as the old legends had said, by the strangers coming out of the east.

And the choice was diminishing. Beg for food from the Wasichus or hunt game that soon would not be there.

But for Crazy Horse and his warriors and the women never far from them, there was yet only one trail, the one of the plains. The year 1875 was the last year of peace, but it was a bad peace, because already the agency chiefs, Spotted Tail and Red Cloud and the rest, were being threatened with stopped supplies if they held out any longer in selling the Paha Sapa, and even all the lands between the Paha Sapa and the Bighorns, so that the good buffalo country of the Powder and Tongue Rivers and the Rosebud would be gone from the Lakota forever. Lots of money, many presents, enough food for everybody for seven generations, the commissioners said, as if this were real value for that sacred land! Be wise, they told the indignant Lakota leaders, meaning: "You are going to lose it anyway, for the armies of the whites can take it from you if they want to, so why not get the money and food and goods now?"

"The Eagles have turned into vultures," said Touch-the-Clouds of Lakota leaders forced into this position. The Minneconjou son of old Lone Horn of the north added: "My father died too soon to see this happen. He went alone into the prairie and died quickly in the strange sacred way, as some of the old ones are doing now to show that death is better than slavery to the whites."

Crazy Horse could only look at his tall friend, whose head topped all the other Lakota, and nod his head. But he could not let his heart sink like a stone. He had to think of the people, and so he counseled with his friend and others about how they could stop this sickness of the spirit.

Then one day Little Big Man came running by in the Moon of the Ponies Shedding Hair, a gun in his hand and shouting: "There is a black robe coming over the grass toward us alone. I am going to kill him. He comes to weaken us with words!"

Crazy Horse lifted his arm commandingly.

"Let him come!" he said. "If we are not strong enough against his words, we are not strong enough for anything." There was a time when the Lakota, close to a trustworthy Mother Earth, had welcomed these black-robed people bearing the sign of their Son born to a Holy Woman, and had accepted them, thinking of their wise Buffalo Calf Maiden. But when these people said the sacred things of the Lakota no longer had power and the Indians must accept the greater power of the white man's religion, the Lakota had looked at their holy hills and wondered. Could these white men be using religion to conquer the minds of the Indians and turn them into slaves, as had already happened in the east?

So Little Big Man had raised his gun, which now he lowered at the words of Crazy Horse, but his short, powerful body bristled with anger as he turned away, spitting on the ground.

"Look out for that one!" Worm warned, as he had done before. "One day he will do us harm with his sudden angers and his too quick finger."

But Crazy Horse watched curiously as the black figure came across the plain, his hand upheld with a wooden cross, its polish gleaming in the sunlight. When the white priest was invited into his tipi, Crazy Horse saw a man of middle years with a thin ascetic face and intense gray eyes that looked on the Lakota warrior without fear.

"*Hou, Kola!*" he said.

"Hou, Kola," replied Crazy Horse. "My lodge is your lodge. My wife will bring you food and drink and you shall find shelter here."

The Black Robe bowed his head and spoke in passable Lakota: "Your kindness to me will be remembered by the Great Spirit. I know your heart is good and that is why I have come to you. I come seeking peace for your people and mine, and also to offer you the help of the Master of Life, Jesus, who is the only born son of the Great Spirit, and who died for us that we might live again. It is Jesus who would have us all be brothers, helping each other in this land. I know also that there are great difficulties because there are bad white people who come to you with lies, who teach your people to use the crazy water that makes them mad, and who try to seduce your girls and women. I know for a truth that for every bad thing the Indians have done to the white people there are ten bad things the whites have done to the Indians. Yet I also know, as you know, that your little ones and your weak ones will be terribly harmed if there is war. And I know, as you must know by now, that the white armies are like the seeds of the grass, and they will come and come until you are no more if you try to fight against them."

"You speak words of wisdom," Crazy Horse replied courteously. "I know about your Master of Life, Jesus, for I have had the traders' sons read to me about him from your Sacred Book. I see from what they tell me that he, like our White Buffalo Calf Maiden, was also a Sacred Being, who has brought the Message of the Great Spirit. If he were here now he and the White Buffalo Calf Maiden would be one to us, and we would surely listen to him and believe in all his words."

"Then," cried the priest with joy, "you must already be a Christian!"

But Crazy Horse shook his head. "Your sacred one foretold, even as did the White Buffalo Calf Maiden, that one day there would be peace between all peoples," Crazy Horse answered. "But I am not a Christian in your meaning of the word, for I believe that all peoples all over the earth have received help from the Great Spirit through Sacred Beings, even as we did, and that if we would listen to the wisdom and goodness all these beings teach us from the Great Spirit, then we would leave the little things that divide us and be brothers in the big things. But your people have forgotten, or they would not be divided as they are so that you confuse the Indian peoples and divide them too, making us leave our Sacred Tree and Sacred Circle for your little squares of religion that rub and irritate each other."

"It is true my people are divided by their

religions," said the priest, bowing his head, "and this is a very sad thing. But you must know that we Black Robes belong to the Catholic Faith, whose very name means unity for all Christians, and once all the Christians had this unity but men came along who divided them up so they are as they are today. Our purpose is to bring them all back together again."

Crazy Horse was silent for a while, making markings on the earth floor of his lodge. Then he lifted his head and spoke slowly: "I know you mean well, my friend, and if other Wasichus could be like you and the few friends we have had among the whites, there would be no trouble between our peoples. But even the one your people tell us is the Great Father does not protect us from the lies and bad actions of those who work under him. You know that it was not many years ago that your people signed a treaty with us that we would own the land of our fathers from the White River to the Little Bighorn and that it and the sacred mountains, the Paha Sapa, would be ours as long as grass should grow and rivers run. But now we know that this was a lie, for they have found gold in our sacred hills and now they want all the land from Paha Sapa to the Bighorns.

"As for your Catholic faith, I am sure it is a good faith for you, and some of you Black Robes have been good to us and helped us. But there are many who call themselves Catholic who do not live up to these things you teach, and they hurt us as much as the other Wasichus by stealing our lands, hunting for gold where they have no right to go without our permission, selling our young people the crazy water, and telling us lies like the rest. So you can see that somehow what you teach is not as big as you say it is, for otherwise these walls between all the groups of Wasichus would not exist and they would be one people in one big religion as we were in the old days when we all followed the White Buffalo Calf Maiden and her teachings. You see, when unity goes from among the people in any religion, then so also goes respect for religion and for the great dreams among both your people and my people. So today your people, like my people, are following little things of the Spirit and not the big things that would bring us together."

The priest thought for a minute, then said boldly: "Yes, but Jesus and His teachings are the big things we are trying to get back to. When we all turn to Him, we will be truly united! Look to the Teacher, and not to the ones who forget His teachings!"

"My friend, you speak truth, but you have left out one thing. It is indeed true that Jesus was as big as the blue sky and as full of light as the sun, for I have heard his teachings, but he is not the only one who teaches this way, or the only Messenger from the Great Spirit. If he were to meet our White Buffalo Calf Maiden I am sure they would be too big for any walls such as are between your people and mine, for they would be one in the spirit. Both he and she said they would return again when the world needed them. But I do not think this means the same person coming back to earth, but that the same Great Spirit speaks through another of

our two-leggeds. If they are to come back in a
new human form it will be because the world
needs something new for a bad time, something they did not teach, else their teachings
would unite the earth. But this is a new age
coming, and a new way must be taught to bring
honor and glory to all people under a new spirit.
I believe it is very possible this new spirit is in
the world now and beginning to grow, because
I have seen it in vision, but you and I will be
dead before it comes here. We can only pray
that it will come soon to help our children's children."

"Cannot you work with me now to bring
peace between our peoples?" asked the priest.

"My friend, you still do not understand me,
but it does not matter. There will be peace in a
few years, but it will be the peace of the conquered and the dead. Your people are like the
great mountainside when it moves downward
in the avalanche, and my people are the animals in the path of that avalanche. I could
indeed make peace with your people as do the
treaty chiefs at the agencies, and then there
would be an end to this war, but it would be a
peace of the conquered ones, and not a true
peace at all. I, too, wish the little ones and the
weak ones did not have to suffer, for I have seen
their torn bodies and heard their cries. But
there is a time when men must stand up and
be counted as men, or the spirit dies. There is
no peace with justice coming from your people
to our people, for your leaders believe we are
like the bugs they can trample beneath their
feet. If we go down like bugs before them, then

we will be remembered as bugs and our people will forget their greatness. We will be slaves in the spirit as well as in the flesh. But if we die with honor, fighting to the end against this great injustice your people bring to our people, then we will be remembered. Here and there some of our children's children, when they are men and women, will lift their heads and each say proudly: 'I am a Lakota; my people fought with courage and honor, and were conquered only because the Wasichus had superior numbers. So our spirit will come back again, and when the new light comes, our people will be in the forefront of the greatest of battles, the battle to unite the great circle of earth and sky and bring justice to all men."

When Crazy Horse was silent, the priest found a new wisdom, for he was silent too, and when he left to go back to the Wasichus he left knowing there was no more to be said.

Chapter 10

The last war cry

In the Moon of Frosting in the Lodge of 1876, word came from the agencies that the soldier chiefs of the Wasichu were demanding that all the holding-out camps come in from the plains and the hills in thirty days or they would be considered enemies. Crazy Horse and many more of those still holding out laughed at this. Even the young and strong with good horses could not make it with their lodges and weak ones in that time of unpredictable weather. Either the Wasichus were mad or they meant to force a war, and it looked like the latter.

But some got frightened for their women and children by the stories of the thousands of soldiers coming into the Lakota country from the east like the swarms of locusts in summer. One of these was He Dog, and it made Crazy Horse's heart sick to see this strong friend of his planning to take his group of lodges in to the whites. But Crazy Horse stood up in the

council and said to let those who worried about
their women and young ones go, for only those
should stay who had strong hearts. So He Dog
left one early morning during a Chinook wind
that had dried snow off the ground of the Moon
of the Dark Red Calves, and Crazy Horse felt
there was a great hole in his heart, joined to
the one left by another strong friend, Young
Man Afraid, when he too had decided it was
useless to fight the whites any more and had
taken some of the Oglalas to the agency at Red
Cloud.

Word came later that He Dog's group had
joined Two Moons and his Cheyennes at the
mouth of the Little Powder when a new snow
came, and they were waiting there until the
weather changed good again before going into
the agency. Then in the middle of the Moon of
Snow Blindness a scout came running into
Crazy Horse's camp with news of people coming, poor and wounded and some walking with
rag-wrapped feet through the snow. Crazy
Horse set up a call for the women to start cooking food and gather spare blankets and clothes,
then led the warriors out to find the Cheyennes
of Two Moons and the Lakotas of He Dog coming in a long, partly broken line out of the
south, a few warriors riding guard on the flanks
and rear. It was a sad story they told of being
struck in the dawn by a company of soldiers
led by Reynolds, a little soldier chief under
Three Stars, as they called General Crook.
Somehow the warriors had managed to get the
women and children off into flight with the
horses, and had fought hard enough to keep

the soldiers at bay until the full escape was made, had even captured some of the soldiers' beef herd in a backlash through the snow, but the lodges had been burned and much food and sacred things destroyed. Now He Dog and Two Moons and their warriors talked no more of going back to the agencies. They were in the fight that was coming in the summer, and in it for good.

As the weather changed and the sun came stronger up from the south, Crazy Horse could feel the spirit of his people growing, and he forgot for a while the dark days foretold in his great vision on Bear Butte. In the Moon of Tender Grass the horses too began to gather strength, as the holding-out Oglalas came together on the plains of the Powder and more of the Cheyennes and others of the Lakotas began to join them. Then the day came when the Oglalas met in council and chose Crazy Horse as their leader, so that a great shouting ran all through the camp, while the drums beat and the women trilled the victory song. "*Hopo!* Let the whites come now!" the warriors cried. "We will make no more mistakes; we have a leader who wins every battle."

Now in the Moon of the Ponies Shedding Hair, with the blue-bright circle of the sky glorious above the waves of emerald grass, the Oglala-Cheyenne camp moved north and west to the valley of the Rosebud, drawn by news that there were good buffalo herds there. First they came to the camps of the Hunkpapas, under Sitting Bull, Gall, and Crow King, and then on together to that of the Minneconjous,

under Lame Deer and Touch-the-Clouds, plus
bands of Two Kettles, No Bows, and Blackfeet,
even Yanktonais, Santees, and, out of the south,
some Blue Clouds or Arapahoes. All these were
gathering in the greatest Indian circle most had
ever seen.

By the beginning of the Moon of Making Fat
the great camp had rolled along to the headwaters of the Rosebud. And there it soon
stretched along the river, further than the eye
could see, with the spirit blowing through it
like a sacred breeze. Here the people watching
the Sun Dance saw Sitting Bull of the Hunkpapas tear a hundred pieces of flesh from his
bleeding arms, fall into a great trance, and
come out of it to say he had seen a vision of
"many soldiers falling into the camp."

Now the young women were hunting turnips
and other wild plants for food on the surrounding swales, and the hunters were bringing in
antelope and buffalo haunches behind their
saddle bows, until the whole camp hummed
with prosperity and joy like a great happy bees'
nest in the first good warmth of summer. It
was a strength too great to be worried by the
reports the runners brought in of armies of
whites gathering to the north and east. The
vast circle had good scouts this time, and there
would be plenty of warning.

And there was something about the way the
warriors tightened their bows and shined their
guns that told Crazy Horse and the other leaders that the Lakotas and their allies were united
and ready for war as never before. He was glad
to have other chiefs listen eagerly to him when

he told of the new methods of fighting the Oglala had developed, rather than curl their mouths down as some of the treaty chiefs did when they felt their power threatened. It was good to see the young men practicing the new way of charging and fighting, some of them pretending they were Wasichus when the war games were played until the shouting and swish and thunder of hooves through the grass sounded almost like a real battle.

Soon again the camp moved over the break of hills to the Greasy Grass or Little Bighorn, and spread along it for three miles or more.

It was an evening warm with the rustle of happy talk around many little fires, and heady with the smell of buffalo and antelope meat cooking, when some Cheyenne scouts came in from the Rosebud with tales of a great army under Three Stars marching there. So the chiefs gathered in council, the young warriors eager for an immediate attack, but some of the older men counseling waiting until the army came near and then forming a wall of Indians against them. Crazy Horse waited until the last of all and when he spoke, his quiet tone and his spirit soothed both the frightened ones and the too-hastily brave, so that they were brought together as one people.

"The camp will need to be guarded and this could be done by the older warriors and chiefs, while the rest of the warriors come across the hills to the Rosebud quietly so as to hit the army of Three Stars when it is all strung out on the trail. When we strike, avoid the strong groups that are gathered to make a stand with fast-shooting guns, and strike the scattered groups that are running or traveling, so that we suck off the others to bring help and so string them out to be attacked by other warriors. When you attack, drive through them as if nothing can stop you. If you do this enough, they will begin to get frightened and some will run. Then is when we can kill most effectively and save our ammunition by using war-clubs and axes."

That night, the Lakota and their allies moved along north of the valley of the Rosebud, resting in the early hours to gather strength. It was dawn of a new day when the scouts went over the ridge toward the big bend of the Rosebud. And here they saw some Crow scouts of General Crook's command coming up the ridge toward them. As the Crows fled backward under the first bullets, howling their warning cries to the long ranks of soldiers far below, the Lakotas and their allies came boiling up to the ridge top until it was black with warriors staring down at the Rosebud and the soldiers. Here Crazy Horse cautioned them all to wait, resting their horses and luring the soldiers up to attack them, so it would be the horses of their enemies that would tire first. And so powerful was the command behind his quiet voice that the eager young warriors obeyed in a way they had not done in other battles.

So it began, the Battle of the Rosebud, when Indian chiefs outthought and outfought a white general, even though the general had more men and they were armed with ten guns to every one the Indians had. In that rough terrain of the high hills it became a big battle of many little battles, mostly hidden from each other, as the Crows and the Rees and other Indian allies of the whites came boiling up one slope while the white soldiers rushed up others, and then the Lakotas and their allies on the ridge tops closed down upon them like a whirlwind, coming quickly and circling with a concentrated force.

Somehow Crazy Horse, first on his pinto, and then later on his bay horse, seemed to be everywhere, his red calf-skin cloak with its white dots flying back from his shoulders, his single feather rising above the small stuffed sparrow hawk that rested on the back of his head, his sacred stone behind his right ear, and his body streaked with the sacred lightning flashes. Later white men who were to write about this and his other battles would laugh at the superstition of the Indian, who dressed himself in such a crazy way. But they would not understand the mighty power in these symbols of the greatness of the spirit that lay behind this man, his courage and fearlessness, his uncanny ability to dodge the bullets that came flying at him from every quarter, his quick mind that seemed to gauge and counter each move of the enemy. To the other Lakotas that day, and to their allies the Cheyennes and the Arapahoes, to see and hear Crazy Horse come up behind them with his cry of *"Hoka Hey!* It is a good time to die!"* filled the blood with fire. To their children and their children's children, the man leading them today could never be killed by bullets or passing years.

His quick commands that struck instantly at

the job each man had to do filled them with a great flash of the spirit and a courage so strong that it led many to deeds of supreme bravery and sacrifice. And always they knew that this Itanca was at every moment where the battle raged thickest, thinking of his wounded men and getting them off the field to safety, by himself or with the help of others. He had also an uncanny ability to seize a carbine or rifle dropped by a dead or wounded soldier, sweep it up off the ground at full gallop, ram out a jammed bullet, put in a fresh one, and pass it on to a surprised warrior whose own gun was past firing. And there were other leaders and warriors that day who did heroic deeds.

General Crook had made one bad mistake early in this battle. He'd fancied that the great Indian camp was only five or six miles around the next few turns of the Rosebud, and had rushed off eight troops of cavalry to attack it. The Indians let these troops pass up the valley, and then closed in to attack those who remained. It was a glorious fight, but by mid-afternoon the weight of fire-power on the white side was beginning to push back the tiring Indians. As they fell back, however, a miracle happened. It was Crazy Horse again coming to the thickest part of the battle, rearing his horse high while the bullets whistled around him, and pointing his finger forward. "Be strong, my friends!" he shouted. "Remember the weak and helpless ones at camp! *Hoka hey!* This is a good day to die!" And he charged almost alone directly at the enemy, his rifle cracking its death song even as he rode. Good Weasel and Black

Bear, Fire Thunder, Bad-heart Bull and Kicking Bear, and others like them took up the cry: *"Hoka Hey!* This is a good day to die!" And suddenly there were no more sullenly retreating warriors, but a great wave that rushed forward upon the Wasichu, gathering power as they saw the soldiers begin to hesitate and turn. Then the Indian allies of the whites, the Rees and Crows, were running away too, and the Lakota war cries filled the valley.

Almost up to Three Stars himself, with his little group of soldier chiefs and traders' sons, the charge of the warriors came. But here the soldiers' lines were suddenly thickening, with reinforcements coming, including the returning troops that had gone up the valley, so Crazy Horse, with a wave of his arm and a shrill sound of his whistle, veered his warriors away in a sudden maneuver that caused the first volley from the bunched soldiers to go wild and the second to come too late.

Now Crazy Horse tried to decoy some of the soldiers into a trap up a turn of the valley, but the howling Crows warned the whites at the last moment, and the maneuver was lost.

Now the bullets were gone, the soldiers in too much confusion behind them to attack, the shoulders of the warriors drooping with weariness, and the sun coming close to the western hills. So Crazy Horse gave the signal and they left for the great camp, knowing they had given Crook a scare he would never forget, and that so many wounded and dead soldiers were left on the field that the thrust of the white army was blunted and thrown back even as the king

bull of the buffalo herd throws back and drives
away the brash young challenger, wounded
and exhausted. And so it was, for the scouts the
next day reported that Crook was retreating,
carefully hauling his wounded out of the Rosebud country, not to be seen again for several
months.

Back at the great camp on the Little Bighorn, the warriors came to sing the hero stories
of the battle, stories of Crazy Horse, but also of
Gall and Crow King of the Hunkpapas, Touch-
the-Clouds of the Minneconjou, and many
wonderful Lakota, Cheyenne, and Arapaho
warriors, especially perhaps the Cheyenne girl
who had galloped her horse into the middle of
the fight where her brother, Chief Comes in
Sight, was surrounded by soldiers. She had
helped him climb onto the horse's back with
one sweep of her arm, and had taken him away
with scarcely a scratch out of the midst of
death, the great praising cries of the warriors
ringing in her ears.

But Crazy Horse took no part in the celebra-
tion or story telling. He was up on a hill smoking his pipe in the far silence, thinking with
pride of his warriors in the battle, but knowing
that this was the last of the great years of his
people and probably only one more battle was
left to be won before the long darkness fell. And
he was thinking already of returning to the
Rosebud fight with some of the boys to gather
lead and powder, abandoned bullets and guns,
for the next battle. And there was a need for
runners to go quickly with soldiers' pay money
to the traders to get more guns and call the

young warriors at the agencies, whose spirits would be lifted at news of the fighting and who could get to the Little Bighorn.

Six days later, the great camp moved across the Little Bighorn River to the west bank, the movement little more than a wave in the days of excitement and joy at being all together and having for a while the sense of the power of earth and sky. So the fires flamed in the twilights while the great stories were told and retold, and the young men and women courted on the edges of the shadows, watched alertly but lovingly by the old women, and the boys and girls played by the river as boys and girls always play but with the sense about them of playing in the midst of the greatest time in their lives, for even the small children had heard that Sitting Bull's prophecy would soon come true of the "soldiers falling into camp."

Never had a summer day seemed so beautiful as that day around noon when the scout came racing down from the eastern hills, shouting across the river to the Oglalas: "Soldiers coming! Soldiers coming!" Through the water he frothed his horse and up the far bank, his own shout suddenly drowned in the great roar of the people awakening to danger, coming up out of the calmness of the blue and golden day, the lazy sleeps of some under packed lodges ended quickly by the noise, the children no longer splashing in the waters, but screaming up the banks, the women who were digging for wild turnips in the fields to the west coming into camp with anxious crying.

Crazy Horse heard the sound, first like a

drone, and then like the talk of the Thunder Beings, and his heart and blood and muscles gathered within him. "They dare to come into our land and our camp and attack us without cause," he told Black Shawl as she hurried to gather his equipment as a good warrior's wife. "Now they shall learn what it means when our people are of one mind. Now the eagles shall gather!" And he had grabbed his weapons and was on his yellow pinto and away like a great wind, his "*Hoka Hey!*" calling the warriors. All about him they were coming, streaks of light in the rising dust, and he could see across the river the great dust clouds where the soldiers were riding. Then he saw that many soldiers had crossed the river and were attacking the camp of the Hunkpapas. Sitting Bull, Black Moon, and Gall were leading several hundred warriors in a stand against them.

From that time on the battle was so much like the first of his great dreams that he almost thought he was dreaming it again. Again there were the screams of horses and men in agony, and the feel that bullets about him were like streaks of light that his body avoided as the squirming eel avoids the spear of the fisherman. Again there was the howling of men in combat and the sharp cracking of rifles, the swish of arrows released from bows. He led his Oglalas to help the Hunkpapas in the first battle against Reno's men at the upper camps, drove them reeling back across the river where the clubs and knives of the Indians wreaked fearful havoc in the bloody waters, until the last body of soldiers escaped to the hills above while Crazy Horse shouted, "Save your bullets, my friends, whenever you can!" Then the cry came from the north of other soldiers about to attack the lower camps.

Now he was riding back hard with his warriors to the north, in time to see a very brave thing, four Cheyennes crossing the river, marching in a row up toward the ranks on ranks of cavalrymen coming down off the ridge in a cloud of dust and firing as they came. But the soldiers stopped, as if amazed at this brave thing, four against three hundred, and Crazy Horse had time to change horses where Black Shawl waited for him as a brave wife should. Then there were five courageous Lakotas joining the four Cheyennes and the soldiers' rifles suddenly puffed their smoke of firing again.

But Crazy Horse had seen that Gall and Crow King of the Hunkpapas, along with more Cheyennes under Two Moons, were crossing the river now to the attack with a cloud of warriors, so he set up the cry *"Hoka Hey!* It is a good time to die!"* to gather the Oglalas around him, and swept off to the north as a leading goose spearpoints a flight of hundreds in the springtime, so that they could catch the soldiers from the rear. Across the river, up the slopes, and around and over the high hill they swept, until they heard the crack of guns once more and saw clumps of soldiers before them, some firing from behind their dead horses and one large group where the soldier chiefs and some of their followers were making a last stand in the dust and blood of war.

Then the Oglalas sprang upon them, as the

mountain lion springs upon the haunches of the deer, and they were through them and over them and charging back again as the whirlwind strikes from many sides at the same time. For a little while there were some of the Wasichus who stood up or crouched, still fighting bravely. And here and there you saw a Lakota or Cheyenne or Arapaho locked together with a white, the two like clawing bears, but it was also like a dream that passed swiftly and was no more. Suddenly Crazy Horse found himself stock still on his panting horse, and all about him a moaning and sometimes a shrill scream of a dying horse, but no more of the crack of guns, the swish of arrows, or the grunts of men fighting. Stunned for a moment at the completeness of their victory, the Indians looked at each other in disbelief. Then the shouts began to rise:

"We have won—the Wasichus are wiped out!"

Slowly Crazy Horse rode down the hill, to make arrangements about the wounded and to see what to do about the remnant of Reno's command, now combined with the company of Benteen and dug in along the ridgetop to the south above the river.

But the next day the great camp was breaking up and moving out, some into the Bighorn Mountains for a hunt and some to the south, for word had come of a new and bigger white army coming up the Little Bighorn, and the chiefs had no more heart for fighting. It was as if they knew the last days of glory had passed and now came the darkness. And this darkness soon rose over the land, after one last blaze of light when the warriors fired all the grass along the Greasy Grass so the horses of the soldiers would have nothing to feed on when they came, the pall of smoke rising to cut out the light of the sun above the Indians fleeing southward.

Chapter 11

"The old songs shall die for awhile"

"When the old songs die, the great dreams are forgotten; and when the dreams are forgotten there is no more greatness!"

Crazy Horse and Sitting Bull had one last talk before the two split up. Sitting Bull headed north with his Hunkpapas and some others, following a devious route to reach Grandmother's Land, Canada. But Crazy Horse would stay in the land of his fathers, as a wounded bear comes back to his mother's cave, for he knew that the Lakotas were wounded deeply, even though they had won the Battle of the Little Bighorn. He put it in words to Sitting Bull: "Our people are full of talk of the great battle, but all their thoughts are in the past, because they know, as we know, that with the death of our brothers, the buffalo, the Lakota too will be a dying people."

"The dark days are coming," agreed Sitting Bull, lowering his wise head toward the earth,

"But I am hoping that in Grandmother's Land we will at least find white men with the straight tongue, and there they do not kill Indians without reason."

"I hope this is true, my friend, but I see only a long blackness coming for all of us before our great-great-grandchildren or their children shall see the light again. For myself, I must stay here in the country of my fathers and try to keep a spark of that light alive in some secret hearts."

The sacred pipe of Sitting Bull, used only at discussions of importance, turned in his strong but sensitive hands. He too had been told in vision that the new greatness would not begin to come until the time of the great-great-grandchildren, he said.

As the older chief spoke, through the mind of Crazy Horse flashed quickly his vision of the time when the Great Spirit would make the whole earth one circle, and men of honor would take the place of those of dishonor. It was to be a time when the earth would be made beautiful again, and the two-leggeds, the four-leggeds, the winged, and all living things would find new life in beauty. Increasingly in the remaining darkening year of his life, Crazy Horse would wish his loved ones were living in those times.

Now, the visionary Sitting Bull, who had earned his name—One Who Stations Himself Between the Enemy and Those He Protects—and his younger chief friend wondered if the Wasichus could change, as the dark shadows fade under the light of the sun in a new morning. Crazy Horse told the older man, "I see a time, after the sky has grown dark and ugly and the waters bad-smelling, when the young white ones will come to those of our people who still carry the spark of knowledge of unity with all that lives and ask for wisdom. In that day there will be some who carry the light and who will give it to them."

For a little longer the two counseled quietly together. Then they smoked the pipe of parting, sending the plumes of smoke to the seven directions, to the east and north and west and south, to Mother Earth and twice up to Father Sky, the last time signifying the sacred connection of man to the Great Spirit.

Soon followed a bad time for Crazy Horse and his followers, a bad time that steadily grew worse, like that of a great wolf, the pack leader, when the hunters are closing in on him from all sides and there are many packs of dogs baying on his trail. One by one his followers go down, until he stands almost alone. And so it was with Crazy Horse, as his first vision had foretold.

It was true there was a killing of his followers by the guns of the white soldiers, or Indian scouts in their pay, as were the Oglala Sitting Bull and four other peace-seeking leaders killed at Fort Keogh by the Crow scouts in the Moon of Popping Leaves. News of the killing of Sitting Bull he was spared—came twelve years after his own violent death. But he saw the cold snowy time on the Tongue River, in the Moon of Frosting in the Lodge (1877), when the soldiers of General Miles, in their warm buffalo coats and many-shooting guns, drove the shiv-

ering Oglala out of the warm bluffs by the
water and over the icy hills. But it was not this
physical killing that really hurt him deep
within; it was far worse to see the spirit of his
people dying as they felt the white men closing
in on them, and the buffalo and elk so hard to
find that often the skin bags of the people were
empty of food. He knew the people loved him
for the way he somehow found game where no
other hunter could find it, bringing in the
blood-dripping haunches and tongues to the
hungry at the time of greatest need, and the
way he comforted the sick and the wounded,
while his strange power made them feel protected in a way no other leader could. But he
saw the deep shadows in their eyes when they
watched him, and no matter how far he twisted
and turned over the plains and hills to dodge
the white armies, no matter how he tried to
teach the people that this earth was theirs and
the Wasichu had no right to it, he knew those
eyes, even the most loyal, were saying, "How
long must we go on this way when there is no
hope?"

So in the beginning of the Moon When the
Ponies Shed Their Hair, with the green grass
thick again in the hollows and the antelope
flashing their white rumps over the distant
plains, Crazy Horse led his band to a meeting
with Red Cloud and others of those friendly to
the whites. Here Red Cloud and his people
brought with them many presents and many
promises from Three Stars, General Crook,
that the holding-out camps would be furnished
with an agency of their own and all the food

and clothing they needed if they would give up the war and come in. So Crazy Horse agreed, for the sake of his people, having a little flash of hope that maybe with peace, things would be better for them, and that he could fight with his wits instead of guns for justice.

But he soon saw, at the agency at Crow Butte under Red Cloud and the little soldier chief named White Hat, how vain that hope was. He came in with his seventeen hundred men, women, and children, the warriors riding proudly behind him and singing the great Lakota Song of Peace so loudly that even some of the Loafers about the Fort took it up too and sent the echoes from the hills. Even then there was quick evidence as to who were his friends. The soldiers took away the horses from the new arrivals and passed them out among the friendly Indians. How eager then came these other Indians, who had given up the fight long ago, to claim their spoils of war!

"Like the wolves coming to take the meat from the dying bear," said Little Hawk, the uncle who had taken the name of the long-lost brother.

And from that moment on, the snakes of gloom coiled themselves closer and closer about Crazy Horse and his people. The whole atmosphere at Crow Butte was dark with unseen but deeply felt jealousies, bitter words told behind men's backs, and the constant scheming for power and money. He saw it in the whispers behind a held-up hand. He felt it in the hostile glances from other leaders. Worst of all was the helplessness and being forced to stay in

one place doing nothing, as if they were locked
in the cages they were told the white men kept
wild animals in in the city. He would go to
council with White Hat about this useless waiting and their need for an agency, but the words
of the Wasichu would run over the hills of the
wars that were past and leave the valleys of the
present unheard from, making Crazy Horse feel
he was talking with a shadow when it came to
the important things needed now.

Even when General Crook came, and there
was a surge of hope that this Three Stars would
do something with his power, the surge died like
a little whirlwind on the plain. When Little
Hawk, who represented Crazy Horse, spoke
straight to the general's face and reminded him
of promises he had made to find an agency in
the north country for Crazy Horse and his people, Crook turned a dark glance on the stern
old Indian and promised instead a last hunting
trip to the north to get buffalo. Crazy Horse
would have thought Three Stars as bad as the
gray men who robbed the Indians, if he had not
found out later that Three Stars did try hard to
get that agency for the former holding out people, but was stopped by higher orders; probably
from General Sheridan, who openly hated all
Indians. Yet what good were promises that
could be taken away so easily? The powers
among the Wasichu evidently thought the Indians could be treated like meadow mice tram-
pled under the hooves of the buffalo.

But worst still was the great lie of Grabber,
the half-breed interpreter, a man who had fled
to both Sitting Bull of the Hunkpapas and to

Crazy Horse, seeking protection when he had to run from the Wasichus because of killings. Now this man, who had been taken as a friend into the lodges and fed from the stewpots and the grill sticks, was working to build hatred toward Crazy Horse and his people among Wasichus and Lakotas alike. Was it because the treaty chiefs and the Loafers about the Forts had become frightened over the rumors that Crazy Horse might be made chief of all the Lakotas, and were using Grabber to build this poison against him? Crazy Horse lay on his buffalo robe in his lodge and stared up at the little patch of blue sky through the open tent flap and wondered how else it could be explained that Grabber had told the little soldier chief, White Hat, that Crazy Horse had said he would "go north and fight until every white man was killed." How weary he was of this web of lies that surrounded him, the stink that lay over this permanent camp like an ugly cloud, this enforced idleness of his people when they had been used to a changing view of the wide sweep of the plains and the water rushing by from the hills, the song of the meadowlark and the clean beauty of the rainbow.

As he looked at the bit of blue above him, his spirit tried to go up and up out of the tipi and into the wide space of the sky. "*Wakan Tanka,* Grandfather," he called softly, "have pity on us, a broken people! Free us from this trap of the Wasichus; make us live again." And far up in the deep blue he saw a white-throated swift dip and swirl like a leaf caught in a whirlwind, then fly straight up like a bullet going into the farthest depths of heaven. And this sight of a creature of the Great Spirit who still had the freedom he had lost somehow gave him comfort and strength, so that a voice seemed to murmur within him like an echo of all his great visions, saying: "There is still the circle of heaven and earth. Yet a little waiting for your people, then what the Wasichus bring will be only a bad dream that shall pass away like a shadow that has never been. In that day some of the Wasichus too will learn the meaning of the Sacred Circle, and they will help your people change the earth to beauty."

For a moment he felt a flow of glory, a warm feeling all around him, and then he heard the stifled sound of Black Shawl, trying to hide her coughing under her blanket, and he knew again the deep sadness of the time in which he lived.

I shall die, he thought, in a time of darkness, but I shall at least die like a man and know that someday the light will come to my people again.

Perhaps he saw what was just around the corner.

Red Feather, the younger brother of Black Shawl, came galloping to Crazy Horse's camp one day with bad news. Woman's Dress, the son of Bad Face, had added another lie to that of Grabber. He had told Three Stars that a scout had listened outside the lodge of Crazy Horse and heard Crazy Horse tell his subchiefs they would take sixty warriors at the coming council and suddenly attack the soldiers, killing all of them. "And," said Red Feather, "there are Indians now planning to come kill you to get favor with White Hat and Three Stars."

Brother Lakotas coming to kill me for the sake of power! he thought. It is indeed as my dream told me. He began planning on how to get Black Shawl to her relatives at the Spotted Tail Agency before he would be ready to die.

Two days later Crazy Horse started for the Spotted Tail Agency with Black Shawl and two warriors, Shell Boy and young Kicking Bear, the brother of Black Fox.

Where now were the clouds of warriors that once had followed the Strange Man into battles at the Rosebud and the Little Bighorn? Instead the little group heard shouting far behind them where No Flesh, with thirty armed Indian Scouts, and No Water with twenty-five more, were hot on their trail, trying no doubt for the reward offered for the death of Crazy Horse. But Crazy Horse still had his canny knowledge of horses and of battle, and he galloped his group down the slopes and walked them up the hills on a route that kept them always ahead of the warriors who followed.

He knew somehow that this was his last time of freedom, and so he drank into his nostrils the keen air of the Moon When the Calves Grow Black Hair, drank into his eyes all the sights of earth and sky, grass flowing away in waves under the wind, the flights of swallows swooping for insects in the swales, the prairie dogs ducking down their den holes as the horses thundered by, and drank in the warm feel of the sun on his skin, and the cool feel of the breeze in his hair. All life was around him glowing and vibrant, the great muscles of his

*horse expanding and relaxing above the legs
that struck the ground before and behind him,
sending their quivering power up to his own
body until he felt for a while as he had in the
freest days of old when he breathed in tune
with the pulse of the free land of the Lakotas.
He knew that this freedom was going from his
people, but he knew also that in some strange
wonderful way it would all come back one day.*

In time he saw ahead the tipis of Touch-the-
Clouds, his tall cousin of the Minneconjous,
and it was Touch-the-Clouds and his warriors
who soon rescued him from the pursuing scouts
of White Hat, driving them off as the Indians
drive the antelope.

When he and Touch-the-Clouds reached the
agency of Spotted Tail at Rosebud, the great
chief of the Brulés came out with a riding cloud
of his warriors, who threatened the Minneconjous until the white officers who were present
thought there would surely be war. But Crazy
Horse rode between the jeering ranks and lifted
his hand in the sign that meant peace, and so
sad and troubled was his face that the warriors
grew ashamed and were still.

Spotted Tail spoke loudly then about this
being his agency and he was in charge if Crazy
Horse came there, and Crazy Horse saw that
even this great uncle of his, who once had
swept a dozen soldiers from their horses in battle, had been forced into guarding his position
of leadership, for white and Indian alike were
eager to grab it. He had learned to outwit the
white agents at their own game and keep his

people alive, but his face showed the tension of one who must hold the reins of two mismatched and highly strung horses.

Crazy Horse had not come to make trouble for him, so he just sat quietly until the little soldier chiefs explained that he could not stay at Rosebud but would have to go back to the Crow Butte Agency. But they promised to help him explain to the big soldier chiefs about the lies that had been told about him.

"Let me leave my wife with her people," he asked them, "and let me rest for one night. Then I will go back." Dark was the feeling when he said this, as he knew that at Crow Butte there awaited him nothing but death.

So it was arranged, and he and his wife went to sleep in the lodge of his tall cousin, Touch-the-Clouds, with the excited, anxious voices of his people about him like a flock of frightened birds in a storm cloud.

At first in the morning, riding toward Crow Butte, he was surrounded mainly by friends, such as Touch-the-Clouds, Lieutenant Lee, Bordeaux, a trader, Swift Bear, High Bear, and Black Crow. But soon more and more Brulé scouts in their soldier coats came riding up, and he knew he was a prisoner among his own people. He remembered the great days of old and that last free ride of his, yesterday, through the glory of the fall hills. "They cannot take from me the earth and sky!" he whispered to Touch-the-Clouds.

Near Crow Butte a messenger came, telling Lieutenant Lee to take Crazy Horse to the office of General Bradley, and Crazy Horse felt the

noose tightening around him as it does around
the rabbit who has tripped the trap on the trail.
And only when he looked far away to the edge
of the earth could he draw strength from the
memory of the days of his youth with Hump,
those happy days of the running horses and
the good smells of the prairie, and the two great
days of his visions, when the Silent One had
spoken to him in the voice of the Sparrow Hawk
and the voice of the wind in the pines and the
cottonwoods. And he wanted to weep, but there
could be no weeping in this dry and dusty place,
where he saw ranks of silent Lakotas on hill
and grassland, where none but a very few who
rode beside him seemed to be friends.

Now both a good thing and a bad thing happened, one right after the other, like two claps
of the thunder. He Dog came galloping up on
his bareback horse and reined in beside him to
shake his hands with a *"Hou Kola!"* and a
straight, warm look that made him a full friend
again. But at the fort Little Big Man rushed up
not as a friend, but as an enemy, hissing words
of hate in his ear and jerking his arm. Yet
Crazy Horse was too tired even for shock, and
he merely turned and walked into the office
where he thought General Bradley was waiting
for him, hearing the rising tide of hundreds of
voices outside, the sounds full of curiosity and
wonder but also with a note of fear as if the
Lakotas felt that something bad was going to
happen, something they did not want to be
affected by because of their fear. And all over
the land a darkness was growing, as the night
came near, but strangely it was as if a differ-

ent and terrible darkness were riding in from
the east like a great herd of black horses, invisi-
ble horses, but permeating the air with sick
screams and hate-filled eyes. Crazy Horse
looked up suddenly as if he felt their presence,
and was searching the darkening sky to see
them, but there was only Crow Butte looming
to the north and the dull gray streamers of
clouds from which the light was fading.

Then he was inside the office and Lieutenant
Lee was telling him apologetically that General
Bradley had no time to see him now, as it was
getting late, but that he would be safe and could
go now to rest for the night. There was something twisted about the face of the white officer, as if he were in pain and had been forced
to say something he did not believe.

"Hou!" *the Indians around Crazy Horse said,
and rose to go, but Crazy Horse said nothing,
rising as one in a dream to step out into the
fading evening, an evening with no color in
the sky, but only a dead grayness that had no
sense of goodness anywhere, as if somehow
earth and sky had forgotten they were once
warm and beautiful. And it is often in such a
time that the wells of despair and conflict sim-
mering in some men come boiling to the sur-
face in a brief moment of violence to destroy
something as wonderful as the rainbow and as
fine as the dawn.*

*Crazy Horse sensed that Little Big Man was
part of the permeating sickness that surrounded him, and wondered for a moment
why this once strong warrior whom he had
trained was now against him. And he sensed*

also that his few friends who were near were
paralyzed into a strange inaction, for none now
touched his arm or spoke to him words of
encouragement, and he felt as alone as a man
would feel who was lost in a vast and hostile
sea. But an inner strength made him step
firmly forward toward where he was being led.

He walked past a soldier who was walking up
and down with a gun over his shoulder, a gun
tipped by a bayonet, and through the open door
of a building that was strange to him. Now suddenly he saw the bars in the windows and the
men lying against the walls with chains on
their legs, and the blood rushed out from his
heart in a great wave of anger at this treachery.
He turned and as he turned he drew out his
knife, the blade flashing in the last light, his
whole body violent like that of a mountain lion
when the noose falls over its head. But the
powerful Little Big Man seized him from behind
by both arms, and the two swayed and wres-
tled like one living creature. Incredible force
lashed through his body to drag the much
stronger man out the open doorway, while he
growled over and over, "Let go of me! Let go of
me!" Then with a tremendous jerk he was free,
and Little Big Man staggered off with blood
running down his arm.

But other Indians seized him now in powerful hands, and the officer of the day was screaming: "Stab him! Kill him! Kill the bastard!"

There was a rending sound behind Crazy
Horse, caused by the guard stabbing the door
with his bayonet by mistake in his hurry. Then
the steel was wrenched out and went plunging

into the back of the struggling captive like a lance into the back of a buffalo. There was one more such lunge, the sound of steel in flesh sickeningly soft, and then the voice of Crazy Horse calling quietly, "Let go of me, my friends! You have hurt me enough."

A silence seemed to hang in the air like that which follows a mighty clap of thunder, and the hands that clasped the prisoner dropped from him suddenly so that he staggered and sank to the ground, already covered with his own blood. Where before there had been hate, there was now suddenly a shame and a fear that made many run from the scene with faces blank and staring, their hearts cold and heavy as frozen lead. For both hate and fear had been as heavy in the atmosphere that day as the smoke cloud of terrible fire, and yet somehow now all knew, even the sickest of those present, that a great man was dying because some of them had done nothing to save this Itanca from what others of them did to him.

Crow Butte and the upper White Earth country that surrounded it were soon in darkness while many men thought about that day. Some of Crazy Horse's friends were so wild with grief and anger that others had to restrain them. Some just held their heads in their hands, waiting and waiting, the grief building deep inside. Many remembered now the good and kind things Crazy Horse had done and his great leadership in battle, and numbers thought of his honesty that would not let him compromise with the Wasichus.

He Dog, when allowed to go to the wounded

man, put a red blanket over him, and Touch-
the-Clouds, alone of all the former friends, had
the guts to walk through the ranks of soldiers,
like a great ship through the waves, and stand
beside his friend, giving up his gun when asked
to do so, but saying: "You are many, I am only
one, yet I will trust you!" shaming the little soldier chief so that he walked away with head
bowed.

The angry army doctor came at this time to
take charge, furious that nothing had been
done by others to stanch the wound and instinc-
tively smelling treachery and rottenness in the
whole shoddy affair.

"This is no place for him!" he roared. "We
must get him moved to a better room, where he
can be kept warm." So Crazy Horse was moved
to the adjutant's office nearby by several strong
and gentle hands, moaning and growling at
enemies he still felt hovering around him, but
gradually quieting under the doctor's sleeping
medicine. Here only Touch-the-Clouds was
allowed to sit with him. *And far away over the
land in darkness there seemed to come a soft
moaning song, as of many women keening over
the death of a beloved. And in that darkness
there were some who sought angrily for Little
Big Man, remembering the great dream of
Crazy Horse that he would be killed only when
held by the hands of one of his own, and
remembering that other time when Little Big
Man had held him when No Water had shot
him with his pistol. But Little Big Man was far
away by now.*

Later that night Worm, the father of Crazy

Horse, came like a shadow out of the darkness, his wrinkled face pinched with sorrow, his hand seeking that of his son, and his words calling into the gulf between them: "My son, my son, I am here!" But only the deep breathing answered him, and he had to wait through the long, long hours of that night, hoping for words that never seemed to come.

In the darkness before the dawn Crazy Horse stirred and the father bent forward, hearing a rattle starting in the breathing, seeing the eyes open slowly, at first seeing nothing, then settling on the familiar old face that bent near.

"My son, I—am—here!" the broken words came.

The dying man focused his eyes painfully on that wrinkled, weathered face. Then those eyes filled with a sudden but quickly fading glow and he whispered, "My father. You see I am hurt. Tell my people they can hear my voice no longer."

The father bent still closer, but the wide-open eyes seemed to be staring sightlessly now, and some of the long brown hair slid gently to the floor till Touch-the-Clouds lifted it with a touch like a mother's, raising it to the dead man's chest. Then the two heads of the living bent lower and the tears fell from their eyes as the springs of the mountains of the west send their waters on their way to the far-off sea. Unashamed tears were these that must flow to join the shining waves of the Great Spirit that wash over the heroes who have died after lives of courage, of dedication, and of love.

Chapter 12

The Crazy Horse monument

Some five miles north of Custer, in the Black Hills of South Dakota, one of the greatest rock carvings ever produced by man is taking shape, carved from the solid granite on seven thousand-foot-high Thunderhead Mountain. The final form, which will be more than five hundred feet high and more than six hundred feet long, will be of the great Sioux war chief and holy man, Crazy Horse, riding a wild stallion, his arm pointed to the east. The bulk of it will not be a bas-relief, but a whole gigantic mountain bitten out by chisel and dynamite into the greatest statue of a man and horse ever produced, larger than all four great heads of the presidents at nearby Mount Rushmore. Below the massive carving will be cut the significant words, said to an army officer who mocked Crazy Horse in his defeat, "My lands are where my dead lie buried."

In late June 1969 I was privileged to be

165

taken by the sculptor, Korczak Ziolkowski, on a ride in his jeep up an extraordinarily rocky and steep road to the top of the mountain and around it to see what had been done on this statue. Mr. Ziolkowski is a giant in size and spirit, bearded and fiery-eyed as an ancient prophet of Israel, literally fulfilling the deep call of John Muir, "Give me men to match my mountains!" Jounced and jerked along that incredible road, the jeep sometimes seeming ready to buck over backward, and shown on the mountaintop the titanic results of the movement of two and a half million tons of rock by dynamite and bulldozer in what have been only the preliminaries to the job, I could feel a thrill of wonder tingling through every vein and artery. How could even such a giant of a man have visualized and then had the temerity and guts to carry out such a super-human undertaking? No wonder many of the people of the Dakotas laughed at him and called him crazy, few believing that there was the slightest chance of his ever finishing such a job. In those beginning years, he had to climb the cliff by rope ladder, marking off the lines of the monument with hand chisel, the work proceeding so painfully slowly that it would obviously take generations to complete. But his grim determination, imaginative self-reliance, and invention started a snowball of effort rolling that graduated him to the jeep road, to two immense electric compressors that produced enough air for all the drilling, to helpers with jackhammers, to a sixteen-ton bulldozer that I saw in furious action under the hands of his son, Johnny, and finally to a gigantic forty-ton bulldozer ready soon to handle the biggest boulders and hurl them over the cliff. So his goal of completing the monument by the end of summer, 1977, the hundred-year anniversary of Crazy Horse's death, now seems possible.

The government offered him financial help if he would turn the work into a National Monument, but he turned them down, his faith borne out by the money that began to roll in. Great upon the Mountain indeed will be this mighty statue of Crazy Horse, and Great upon the Mountain also will be written in stone the convictions of Korczak Ziolkowski.

The monument is now under the control of a nonprofit corporation, dedicated not only to creating the monument, but also to founding a University of North America where Indian culture would be taught and stimulated. It was due to urging by Indians that Ziolkowski built the monument; after he returned to Connecticut from having worked at Mt. Rushmore with sculptor Gutson Borglum, Chief Standing Bear wrote and asked him to carve a mountain "so that white men would know that the red men had great heroes also."

Later he was approached by a delegation of Indians, who told him the Black Hills, or Paha Sapa, were the Sacred Mountains of the Indians and should never have been formed into the heads of white presidents. Struck to the heart by their words and their depth of feeling, he promised to carve a great Indian on one of the mountains. But the first mountain he selected for a hundred-foot-high statue somehow could not satisfy him. Some strange power seemed to be driving him to find a place where he could carve something far larger.

When he saw Thunderhead Mountain, his eye instantly filled that massive granite cliff with a giant figure rushing forward on horseback, his arm uplifted and pointing. When he measured out the actual space it would take to do the job, even his glowing optimism was dampened and he wondered how he could ever meet the challenge. But something drove him relentlessly to try.

Something called him from that peak, lifted
and then filled his eye with a picture in
the sky,
Of a chief who warriors led through the val-
ley of the dead, where the bullets scream-
ing fled;
Fought to hold this golden land where the
grasses rolled in flame and the bisons'
herd bulls came;
Knew the thrill of victory won, at the Rose-
bud threw back Crook, joined the whip-
ping Custer took,
Till the Little Bighorn's waves turned blood-
red from bank to bank, and the troopers
fell and shrank.
Yet there was a greater call than this tale of
blood and gore, something where the
eagles soar,
Something of a vision seen where the Thun-
der Beings dream and the wind is calling
keen;

While he saw his folk go down, like the grass,
    hoof-beaten brown, when the dark herds
    crossed the crown
Of the hills that ring the plain; knew his peo-
    ple lived in pain while the warriors now
    lay slain;
Still his eyes, long-seeing born, looked ahead
    beyond that doom to a light that broke
    the gloom.
To the Wakan-holy gleam of a time when
    spring would come, spirit-springtime
    with a drum,
Rolling thunder down the hills where the
    birds are lilting trills and the prairie
    chicken drills.
What drum beats with such a sound, deep as
    thunder yet so round, joyous as a heart
    unbound?
Hear it, see it, by a tree; sacred, holy is that
    tree, growing leaves to make men free.
Tree of Understanding know, by the way its
    flowers glow, by the thrilling tremolo
Of the voices raised in praise in that day
    when shadows fade and all races, un-
    afraid,
Dance the circle dance of love, as they hear
    the One Above call them up, led by a
    dove.